Beyond Utility

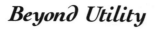

Beyond Utility

Liberal Education for a Technological Age

Athanasios Moulakis

University of Missouri Press

Columbia and London

Copyright © 1994 by
The Curators of the University of Missouri
University of Missouri Press, Columbia, Missouri 65201
Printed and bound in the United States of America
5 4 3 2 1   97 96 95 94

Library of Congress Cataloging-in-Publication Data

Moulakis, Athanasios, 1945–
  Beyond Utility: liberal education for a technological age /
  Athanasios Moulakis.
     p.   cm.
  Includes bibliographical references (p.) and index.
  ISBN 0-8262-0929-7 (alk. paper)
    1. Education, Humanistic—United States. 2. Science—Study and
teaching (Higher)—United States. 3. Technology—Study and teaching
(Higher)—United States. 4. Education, Higher—United States—
Curricula. I. Title.
LC1011.M76   1993
370.11'3'0973—dc20   93-27212
                                                                 CIP

⊗™ This paper meets the requirements of the
American National Standard for Permanence of Paper
for Printed Library Materials, Z39.48, 1984.

Designer: Elizabeth K. Fett
Typesetter: Connell-Zeko Type & Graphics
Printer and Binder: Thomson-Shore, Inc.
Typefaces: Sabon, Collage

This book is brought to publication with the generous assistance of the
Publications Program of the National Endowment for the Humanities,
an independent federal agency.

For E. G. M.

Contents

Acknowledgments ix

Introduction 1

Part 1
Doing Things Right—and Learning the Right Things to Do:
    Liberal Education for Engineers

  1. Speaking One's Mind 9
  2. A Manly Profession 13
  3. Second Thoughts: The Needs of Advanced Industrial
     Societies 19
  4. Literacy and Democracy 23
  5. Technology and Freedom 26
  6. Efficiency vs. the Love of One's Own 30
  7. Cultural Literacy 32
  8. Of Content and Form in Teaching 36

Part 2
The American Way in Liberal Education

  9. The Tower of Babel 41
10. *E Pluribus Unum?* 44
11. Diversity and Its Discontents 49
12. "O! that the Everlasting had not fix'd His canon 'gainst
     self-slaughter!" 54
13. Innocents Abroad 60
14. Manifest Destiny vs. the Serpent Columbus 65
15. Babylonian Captivity and the Suffering Servant 69
16. Separation as Collective Therapy 74

17. The Crustacean Theory of Culture 77
18. Herstory? 82
19. Conformity and Individuality 85

Part 3
The Confusion of Tongues

20. What Is the Tower of Babel For? 91
21. A Scientific Morality? 94
22. Two Cultures? 100
23. The Retreat from the Word 104
24. Teaching Values 110

Part 4
A Program

25. Courses of Study 117
26. Humanist Education 120
27. The Civic Mission of the University 122
28. Opportunities and Constraints 125
29. The Text-Based Seminar 131

A Last Word 141

Notes 145

Works Cited 159

Index 167

Acknowledgments

In the process of preparing this book, I have incurred many debts. Sandy Lakoff read the manuscript, made valuable suggestions and saved me from many errors. For helpful comment and encouragement I am grateful to David Riesman. Harvey Mansfield contributed useful remarks. Conversations with Maurice Cranston have had a lasting effect. The students no less than the tutors at St. John's College, Annapolis, made me aware of things about teaching and learning that I had not realized before. For important assistance in word and deed on several occasions I am indebted to Mortimer Adler. Clancy Herbst's generosity made the University of Colorado Humanities for Engineers program possible, and I am happy to say that he continues to take a benevolent interest in it. It has been a pleasure to work with Dave Clough, for whom education is a true calling. I greatly appreciate the support and encouragement my program and I have received from Dick Seebass, Dean of the Colorado University College of Engineering. I welcome the opportunity to recognize Leland Giovannelli's unfailing professionalism and her extraordinary gifts as a teacher. Cindy Bogner must be praised, not only for her competence as an administrative assistant to the program but for the rare gift of being able to read my hand. The book is dedicated to my best friend.

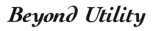

Beyond Utility

Introduction

The modern world lives by the products of technology. Technology, in turn, depends on human ingenuity; high technology depends on highly trained ingenuity. Consequently, industrial society has come to depend less on things like physical labor, land or industrial plants as such than on the trained and informed minds of people. Education, and higher education in particular, has become, in this instrumental sense, the pivotal institution of the modern world. It is important, therefore, to ask ourselves if it is doing what it ought to do if only because the ingenious technological processes and products of modern science, or their real and potential by-products, also threaten to destroy our world. Fears of nuclear and ecological catastrophe naturally focus the mind on the necessary limits of human endeavor. But quite apart from that, no education focused on mere survival or devoted to some blind process of growth would be worthy of the name.

We have come to rely on experts in order to get things done right. Expertise is the characteristic, but not the exclusive, quality of the engineer. If, however, expertise is to be transformed into creative ingenuity, what is required is a broader perspective and an elasticity of mind that technical training alone cannot provide. Ingenuity itself cannot furnish its own sense of direction, and the very success of our technical cleverness forces us to come to terms with the possibility of ingenious blunders. Doing the right things belongs to a different order of thought than doing things right.

The education of engineers is widely perceived as being too narrow, not least by engineers themselves. Engineering attracts bright people and equips them to do important things, but it does little to help them understand the human condition or, indeed, the fullness of their own humanity. It would be foolish, however, in my view, to deny engineers the technical education they need in a misguided effort to make them "more rounded" when a great deal can be done not so much by diluting engineering curricula as by rethinking the portion devoted to liberal studies. This book concludes with the outline of a program that can serve as an example of how this can be accomplished. Central to this program, beyond well-focused, eye-opening introductory lectures, is

1

the enlisting of a dedicated faculty to teach the students to think and express themselves by reading and discussing well-chosen texts that explore the ever-recurrent issues of meaning, aesthetic sensibility, and morality. Uncompromisingly dedicated to traditional standards of learning and scholarship, the program is as concerned about the manner as it is about the content of the course. It is conceived as an exercise in articulate humanity and civic responsibility, as well as a reflection on human artifacts, performances, and achievements.

An education does not consist of turning the candid gaze of the student from one object to another with images of a more or less complex reality registering on a photographic plate. It is rather the active transformation of a mind—or, more generally, of a sensibility—as it seeks to attain a higher degree of discernment and greater coherence within the universe of meaning it inhabits. An education is, therefore, never a mere acquisition, be it of tools or of objects of knowledge, but the maturation of an understanding and the heightening and refining of the desire to know. The objects of knowledge are important, of course, and no education would be possible or even conceivable without them. But the objects of knowledge are not, as it were, the substance of knowledge. As Dante's Francesca says of her love to Paolo, which was sparked by the reading of poetry, "The book and he who wrote it was the go-between," whereas what really matters is the ardor it occasioned.

In this book, I will argue that a liberal education cannot be obtained as the direct object of a deliberate effort, that it is rather the side effect of efforts which prove to be indirectly conducive to making a human being civilized; its lessons cannot be taught like a precept or a set of rules but can only be imparted in roundabout ways.

Abstract reflection and the acquisition of material knowledge are indispensable and valuable in themselves; a liberal education has something of both, but it is neither a mere skill nor a hoard of treasure. Even the image of growth, though less misleading, is limiting, for it suggests a predetermined end, similar to a fully grown oak tree accomplishing and exhausting the possibilities enclosed in an acorn. The fruits of a liberal education, i.e. the good use of human freedom, though never unconditional, are not determined at the outset.

These reflections suggest limits to the effectiveness of education as an instrument of narrowly conceived—its proponents would say "focused"—public policy. A certain rationalist optimism tends to trust the direct effects of instruction. The schools then seem to provide a handy lever to bring about what one takes to be socially desirable ends without grappling with the more intractable problems of social reform.

The results are generally disappointing, from a social as well as an educational point of view. A more modest view of what education can effect directly and in the short run seems to me to agree with a grander view of what education can achieve in the long run, i.e., create the conditions of possibility of human creativity. This latter achievement is, however, notoriously difficult to assess in terms of cost-benefit analysis, and therefore difficult to sell, especially to those responsible for short-term budgets. This book is also intended as a sales pitch for the broader vision, in the interest—as I hope will emerge—not only of a fuller and more humane life but also of common utility.

Education does not merely inform; it forms the student. The various modes of human learning can only come together in *the person* of the student who is accordingly changed by learning. The difficulties of integrating human knowledge, the fracturing of the world of understanding—even within the ostensibly coherent sphere of science—into discrete cultures that fail to communicate, and the weakening of language itself, are discussed in part 3 of the book. These are, I think, the broader and more permanent problems that educational policy needs to confront. These issues seem to me inextricably linked with the workings of the modern world, as it is formed by the development of science and technology.

It has become impossible to separate technology from science. Traditions of workmanship, hands-on tinkering and direct familiarity with a world of artifacts undoubtedly continue to inform technical creativity. There is no denying, however, the increasing importance of applied science to technological innovation. From polymers to the atomic bomb, there are countless technical accomplishments that are unthinkable except as applications of science, which no amount of empirical know-how could ever have brought about.

But it is conversely quite possible to separate—at least conceptually—science from technology: a science conducted at a distance from applications (though often dependent on technological apparatus for its experiments); a science driven by the desire to know and only indirectly and often fortuitously linked to possible applications. Yet even here, problems of responsibility arise, because discoveries have consequences, especially in a world in which discoveries can be transformed into powerful inventions.

To what extent can—or should—scientific inquiry resist the pressures of its techno-logical/utilitarian surroundings? What, under our present predicament, are the conditions of free scientific inquiry of the kind that make science a liberal pursuit?

In order to clear the ground for these issues, I discuss in part 2 a different set of problems, which bear on the conditions of intellectual liberty and the highly contentious questions regarding the degree of social and cultural cohesion necessary for a civilized society to function. These considerations naturally bear again on the kind of preparation a university education can and should provide.

On the whole there is, I believe, reason for cautious optimism: despite the tensions that arise between the aims of a rounded, humanistic education and those of the specialized training required by competent professionals; between the demands for the efficient organization of means and the need for the personal articulation of meaningful ends; between—to oversimplify—the promise and the risks of technology, it is, I believe, more nearly possible in the present state of advanced industrial society to aim for an educational program that tries, in Rousseau's words, "always to bring together what right permits with what interest prescribes so that justice and utility are in no way divided."[1] Such coincidence is, of course, far from automatic, but it is, I think, quite possible and certainly worth striving for. Any upright person will, if necessary, sacrifice utility (i.e., apparent utility) to justice, but a society is far more likely to see that the right things are done if they also seem evidently useful. In part 1 of the book I hope to show how agreement between justice and utility is possible in our day.

What I mean by a liberal education will emerge, I hope, more clearly from the book as a whole. No education can be separated from substantive knowledge or the acquisition of a number of skills. Some subjects or disciplines are, no doubt, naturally more conducive to a liberal education than others. But the liberal education I seek to promote is not so much the command of certain materials over mastery of others. Nothing is further from my mind than the idea of "liberal studies" as a residual category for disciplines that are not vocational, technical, or scientific. "Liberal" is an adjective, and it refers to a quality, not to a substance. A liberal education may well be compatible with and, as I have suggested, may even actively further the pursuit of utility. But what makes it liberal is that it is its own reward. The product cannot be divorced from the activity. In this sense, science can be a liberal pursuit of the highest order. Any discipline, on the other hand, conventionally classed with the "humanities" or the "social sciences" may be pursued in a servile spirit.

A liberal education is not content with establishing the appropriate means to given ends but constitutes an inquiry into the ends themselves and is thus an end in itself. It is concerned with the realm of value, and it is predicated, in turn, on the idea that value is rooted in human freedom. One can be forced to obey commands, but values one has to hold for oneself: enforced values are not really values at all. A liberal education is constituted, then, in the tension between the two propositions that the truth shall set you free and that you need freedom in order to see the truth.

The reflections that follow were occasioned by the founding of the new and innovative program of Humanities for Engineers at the University of Colorado, Boulder, in the fall of 1989. In order to make sense of our undertaking I found it necessary to view it in a broader context. I was therefore led to explore the more general subject of liberal studies and their place in professional education. This, in turn, gave rise to yet broader reflections on the nature of liberal education and on its role in modern society. Since my primary practical concern was, nonetheless, the humane education of engineers, many of my examples were drawn with an eye to that particular field.

The problems of providing engineers with a rounded education are not new. They are perhaps more urgent than before, but they have been present since the establishment of formal engineering education in the mid-nineteenth century. The vocabulary of educators naturally reflects shifts in professional self-understanding and social sensibility over the years. Despite that, the same themes recur with remarkable constancy. Study after study, in the twenties, the forties, the fifties, down to the nineties, each motivated by the perceived crisis of the time—the effects of World War II, Sputnik, foreign competition, the environment, etc.— has come up with a similar analysis of the need to provide both a general and a professional education at the same time. Each has pointed to the contradictions that arise from this double pursuit. The recommendations for action across the decades, all advocating a strengthening of liberal studies, are also remarkably similar. The difficulty, it appears, both conceptual and practical, is with implementing such recommendations.

The reflections that follow seek to show why these recommendations should be taken to heart. I have naturally drawn on the work of others and, in particular, on the results of the successive study teams appointed by professional education associations, which express a consensus on the best approach to engineering education as it emerged and matured.[2] The consensus refers, of course, more to the formulation of general goals, and the identification of obstacles in achieving those goals than to any particular, universally accepted course of action. In this book, I hope to show that the concerns engineers themselves have expressed about an education that will make them not only qualified professionals but also better communicators can best be accomplished by avoiding panaceas and concentrating on what we know works well. Adopting some model curriculum in the vain hope of somehow indoctrinating the young with traditional values and lofty standards of literary appreciation is not the right answer. Neither is the adoption of some more trendy curriculum influenced by this or that notion of what is politically correct or morally desirable. The right approach is to respect students' personal autonomy and to help them learn to become articulate in speech and writing and better able to exercise informed judgment. The best way to do this is through patient and dedicated teaching that sets out with the modest goal of helping students learn to read important texts that deal with aesthetic and ethical issues and to talk about their reactions among themselves. I also trust that the argument advanced here will contribute to the broader discussion on the goals and conditions of educational policy in a truly liberal spirit. The liberal education of engineers is, of course, primarily of interest to them, their teachers, and their employers, but it also affects their fellow citizens and fellow human beings. The issues it raises are indeed emblematic of the problems of a liberal education and the culture of freedom in a technological age.

Part 1

Doing Things Right— and Learning the Right Things to Do

Liberal Education for Engineers

Speaking One's Mind

Engineering is a profession. It requires rigorous and systematically structured training, which leaves little time for the liberal aspects of a rounded education. Unlike the training for other professions, such as law or medicine, engineering education is primarily—and in many cases exclusively—undergraduate education. It is likely to remain so. Engineers, unlike lawyers and physicians, do not benefit from baccalaureate general education prior to their professional training. But what in one sense may appear to be a drawback may paradoxically prove to be an advantage. Studies show that the desired balance of technical and humane educational goals is not best achieved by sequential or "separate but equal" courses of liberal and professional education, but by concurrent, integrated programs.[1] The historically established pattern of engineering education as a predominantly undergraduate education invites us, then, to develop a well-thought-out, coherent plan of liberal studies. In the face of proliferating, unfocused liberal curricula, it can be a welcome challenge to intellectual discipline to develop a course of study that takes into account the economy of time, personal effort and social cost characteristic of engineering schools.

As people with a practical bent of mind, engineers are understandably impatient with educational requirements that they perceive as merely ornamental. The illusion that liberal studies have little substantial or practical value is further encouraged by the way in which engineering students select offerings in the humanities. They often choose courses more or less at random, following a passing curiosity or picking those that interfere the least with the schedule of technical courses or simply choosing those that require the least effort.

Typically, a haphazard selection of social science and humanities courses produces meager educational results. This, in turn, reinforces the prejudice against the value of a liberal education for the human and professional advancement of engineers.

On the other hand, educators who have given serious thought to the formation of engineers have long felt the need for a strong liberal component in engineering education. An engineer who has enjoyed a broad exposure to liberal learning and who has had the opportunity to lay a solid foundation in the humanities will be 1) a fuller and richer human being, 2) a better citizen, 3) a more useful, effective and successful person, and finally, perhaps surprisingly, 4) a better engineer.

It is often not until later in life that the benefits of liberal learning or, conversely, the drawbacks of its absence become acutely felt. Surveys show that recent graduates of engineering schools wish they had taken more technical courses. Alumni of the same schools who have had some ten years of experience in the field regret not having had more schooling in business and managerial skills. Professionals looking back on careers of twenty years or more, finally, are more likely to say that, in retrospect, they wish they had studied more literature, philosophy, and history.

A liberal education is, of course, good in itself, something worth having for its own sake. It is, in many ways, its own reward and the key to a rich, reflective, and articulate life. A university education worthy of the name must provide more than the tools of a trade. It must enhance the student's familiarity with the wealth of human experience and the many modes—scientific, poetic, philosophical, artistic—of human expression. Beyond the instrumental techniques that constitute professional competence, a university education should point toward meaningful purpose. Engineers are trained to do things right. But they, like all responsible human beings, must develop criteria to use in determining whether they are doing the right things.

A liberal education enables an engineer to place his or her know-how in the context of personal and social aspirations. It helps develop a maturity of judgment to guide the engineer's activity as a professional and as a citizen. It provides a breadth of vision that enables the graduate to enter the life of the community as a well-rounded human being and, where the seed falls on fertile soil, it fosters the capacity and the desire for public service.

But if a liberal education is a good, it is also a source of power. Government bodies, shrewd businessmen, and prominent educators have called for a strengthening of liberal learning at all educational levels. They point out that in a rapidly changing world, professionals will need broadly applicable skills and the capacity to adapt if they are to stay abreast of change. With rapid technological innovation, specialized skills become obsolete in sudden and often unexpected ways. Today's, and indeed tomorrow's professionals, therefore, need to look beyond the capacity to accomplish given tasks and solve set problems. They must develop the judgment that permits them to redefine the tasks at hand and to frame new questions as they arise. Changing circumstances will require the opening of new fields of expertise in which there will be no reliable guides. Faced with a lifetime of challenges, students should acquire the skill of acquiring skills, the skill of teaching themselves.

It is an error to believe that all that needs to be known can be taught and that it can be taught at school. College does not produce ready-made educated men and women who can rest on an accumulation of factual knowledge. Instead, it provides students with a mass of useful information, and an opportunity to develop cognitive tools, habits of analysis and understanding, and an elasticity of mind that lays the foundation for lifelong learning.

It is this elasticity of mind that proves invaluable at the highest levels of engineering design and engineering management. At these levels, the capacity to look beyond the successful accomplishment of particular tasks, the ability to look at wholes in such a way as to change the very terms in which a particular technical or organizational problem is posed, is the key to creative engineering and successful management. An agile mind that has learned to envisage many possible answers in a complex environment is better equipped, at the level of synthetic design and management planning, to devise innovative solutions. A broad liberal education fosters the habits of mind and encourages the creative freedom that make imaginative breakthroughs possible. A broad education, then, not only helps students become fuller human beings and better citizens, but it also equips engineers with a heightened ability to do well in the higher reaches of their own craft.

Engineers are trained to reason clearly and accurately, but they are apt to think in terms of problems that have neat, definite solutions. When faced with questions that have no simple and complete answers, they often feel awkward and unprepared; yet problems of this kind are the most common in life. One's personal life and the life of one's society pose questions for which it is not easy to find the one right answer, the reason being that, in many cases, there *is* no *one* right answer. That does not mean that such questions cannot be treated sensibly and responsibly. Engineers are not alone, of course, in their reluctance to come to terms with ambiguity. But they do tend to shrink from aspects of reality they are altogether too quick to perceive as an incoherent jumble beyond the reach of reason. As a result, although engineering has traditionally drawn gifted people, engineers have not achieved the positions of leadership in government and industry in the numbers that their natural capacity and professional competence entitle them to.[2] A 1981 AT&T study found that over a twenty-five–year period liberal arts graduates rose more rapidly through its managerial ranks than those with degrees in business and engineering.[3] This picture agrees with the thirst for the liberal arts expressed by more experienced engineers that we saw earlier. It is worth noting that though business training was no doubt a help to many, in the long run, it was the practical advantage of a broad humanist education that proved to be decisive. This is especially true at the higher levels of corporate management.

Trained to deal with things, engineers are often poorly prepared to deal with people. In corporate life this makes itself felt as an absence of "boardroom skills," meaning, in particular, a weakness in the use of the English language. Poor communication skills have been the most frequent and persistent object of employers' complaints about the engineering graduates they recruit. It is a sad reflection on the state of elementary and secondary education that students reach the university unable to speak and write clear and correct English. Universities must, nonetheless, deal with the problem realistically. It also stands to reason that students who are inclined by nature and training to quantitative rather than verbal skills need particular attention.

Speaking well and writing well become increasingly important, beyond the corporate sphere proper, in an integrated world in which technical projects must be explained, often in nontechnical terms, to clients, officials, and interested citizens. A technical idea, no matter how brilliant, will remain on the drawing board if it is not clearly presented, its various aspects and possible repercussions properly discussed, the case for it persuasively made. Habits of conversational civility and a trained ear for what is said by others are no less important for the thoughtful and competent engineer. This is especially so when, as often happens, engineers become business managers.

But language is more than communication. It is the very tissue of meaning, which cannot be divorced from thinking itself. It is what human beings have in common, without which even the notion of disagreement is meaningless. Mastery of language is not just an instrumental skill; it is a mode of understanding. Lucid speech, even eloquence, is not an ornament, something added to language; it is language doing justice to the speaker's humanity. Consequently, a humane education should consist less of courses *about* language—courses in communication and the like—than of a broad exposure to good writing and of the careful study and thoughtful discussion of outstanding examples of human speech. In language, as in music, it is by listening that one develops a critical and attentive ear.

2

A Manly Profession

There was a time when engineers could do no wrong. The very nature of their work was felt to be creative, constructive, intrinsically positive. Some people, like William Morris, might have worried about railroads defacing pretty romantic valleys, about the decline of craftsmanship and the passing of traditional forms of social solidarity linked to preindustrial patterns of production. On the whole, however, engineers were seen as agents of progress, busy serving mankind by taming nature.[1] Engineers were transforming modern life for the better, increasing productivity and standards of living, improving transport, sanitation, nutrition, etc. The promise of engineering even extended to the realm of war and peace. In the late nineteenth century, expanding commerce powered by vigorous technology seemed to hold out hope of a lasting peace—at least among "advanced" nations, aware of each other's armaments and interested in each other's trade.[2] Even when such hopes of peace were not entertained, robust patriotism, unclouded by the doubts of a later age, could find no fault in the ancient, almost congenital link between engineering and warfare. For it is worth noting that the oldest schools of engineering, like the renowned *École Polytechnique* and, indeed, West Point, are military academies. It goes to show, if nothing else, that engineering was considered an unquestionably manly profession. Engineering, pitting man against the candid forces of nature, rather than against the falsity and deviousness of other men, was literally and therefore, it seemed to follow, metaphorically edifying. Learning to build things was, it was thought, also the best way to build character. Thus, engineering appeared to be the best preparation for all truly useful occupations.

An editorial appearing in the authoritative organ of the industrial community, the *Engineering News and Railroad Journal,* of February 3, 1893, put it as follows:

> The attractiveness of engineering as a profession is greatly increased by the opportunities which it offers for diverging from the strict line of professional work into other and (generally) more lucrative occupations for

which engineering training and practice are an excellent preparation. This results from the fact that engineering is a practical and creative profession, in broad distinction from the older professions, medicine, law and theology, which, at most, are only negatively creative, in preventing the destruction which would otherwise result from men's vices and follies.

The important point here is that expertise in dealing with things is taken to confer aptitudes of greater universality than skill in relating to people. It would be interesting to reflect on the paradox, which is still broadly true, that the successful engineer is the one who is no longer an engineer. As an editorialist wrote in the *Engineering News,*

> In engineering it is rather the rule than the exception for the successful men to be finally tempted out of strictly professional work to become managing officers of public or private corporations, contractors or founders of industrial enterprises. . . . the trained physician or the theologian is rather deterred by his training from success in any other calling than fitted for it. They rarely diverge from the strict line of professional work after entering upon it. The law is more fortunate, since many lawyers become fitted for highly responsible positions at the head of a certain kind of large corporations, while they almost monopolize the political field (but little else).

Representing the spirit of potential employers, the editorialist writes that the ideal engineering school should waste little time with what are patronizingly referred to as "cultural adjuncts," such as literature, history, and foreign languages. The training of the student should be as practical as possible. This is, of course, the pressure exercised in engineering schools down to our own day. Despite some recent changes of attitude at the top of industrial management, employers press for people shaped to fit the given slots in industry, and deans of admissions must compete for students, who are eager to find gainful employment without unnecessary delay. Educators who felt that no student could leave the university without at least a smattering of culture, and therefore introduced liberal studies requirements, were on the defensive from the beginning.[3]

The editorialist of *Engineering News* did, it is true, want more than technical competence from engineering students. He wanted to see something like the development of character, of physical and mental vigor, and of the capacity to work with others in the accomplishment of common tasks. The model is the army, in contrast to the "laxity" of civil schools.

> Whether or not the future ideal engineering school will do anything more than is now done to imitate military schools, and depart from the prece-

dent of the older civil professional schools, by giving its students an incidental training in what we may call the manly and social accomplishments, is a large question.[4]

The attraction of the military model of social organization is also manifest in Edward Bellamy's socialist utopia, *Looking Backward, 2000–1887*, which appeared in 1889 and enjoyed quite a vogue both in America and abroad, and which envisioned a "new industrial army" organized in military fashion.

What is wanted in the way of "social accomplishments" is a sense of mess hall companionship—grit and efficiency in distributing practical tasks and the appropriate giving and taking of instructions and orders. What are certainly not called for are foppish social graces or airs of cultural refinement, viewed as mere baubles at best, but also as exclusionary devices, as undemocratic and downright effete affectations. The ideal engineer is a regular guy, a red-blooded American who stirs his coffee with his thumb. He is a doer, not a talker. "Taciturnity," announces our editorialist proudly, "is a natural characteristic of a good engineer. His calling is to do things—he has no practice in talking." The student should be given "as practical an equipment as possible; to send him out into the brambles of this world with a stout suit that will stand wear, not equipped merely in holiday attire, only fit to shine on the rostrum on graduation day."[5]

Such language is consistent with the powerful movement creating the new professional schools: engineering, business, and agriculture.[6] Indeed, the spirit of practicality affected the tone of university life as a whole in the context of westward expansion and industrialization. The tendency was, of course, more pronounced in the West than in the East and the land grant colleges provided for by the Morrill Act of 1862 were conceived in this very spirit. It was "part of the larger populist movement which sought to produce the 'undifferentiated American' and through education enable ordinary people to gain prestige and first-class status."[7] In this light the pursuit of utility and populist democratic ideology were juxtaposed to the traditional paradigm of higher education perceived as an ivory tower or, worse, as a device to express and enhance the privilege of men of "good stock" that entrepreneurs like Leland Stanford had so little use for. When he was about to found the university that he would name in memory of his son, Leland Stanford wrote a friend in the following terms:

> I have been impressed with the fact that of all the young men who come to me with letters of introduction from friends in the East, the most help-

less class are college men. . . . They are generally prepossessing in ap-
pearance and of good stock, but when they seek employment, and I ask
them what they can do, all they say is "anything." They have no definite
technical knowledge of anything. They have no specific aim, no definite
purpose. It is to overcome that condition, to give an education which
shall have that result, which I hope will be the aim of this University. . . .
Its capacity to give a practical not a theoretical education ought to be accordingly foremost.

In this vein the classical model of higher education was seen as doubly
reactionary: a) because it was socially exclusive and b) because it re-
tarded the exploitation of America's natural resources and the development of its economic potential. As it happens, Leland Stanford, Jr.,
himself, one supposes, a young man of "good stock" in his father's
estimation, died in Florence while on a cultural grand tour, before he
had the opportunity to become a college man.

The classical model did not just keel over and die. It put up a
vigorous resistance. There are good intellectual reasons for this, for it is
by no means easier to establish what is truly useful than it is to discover
the truth. The pursuit of truth, again, requires a measure of detachment
incompatible with strictly utilitarian pursuits. Consequently, the utilitarian model was not only resisted where the classical manner was
institutionally entrenched, but also countered by innovative educational efforts, producing some of the most interesting educational experiments of our century. On the whole, however, the struggle against
the supremacy of utility as the guiding principle of educational policy—
and engineering education in particular—though often vigorous, has,
until recently, been conducted as a rearguard action, covering a retreat.

Resistance was strongest, of course, where the pursuit of utility was
not seen to coincide simply with a proper sense of values. In varying
degrees, institutions, teachers, and the variously defined communities
supporting them, felt that the ethical norms essential to the rational
pursuit of utility—norms perhaps most familiar from *Poor Richard's
Almanack*—needed to be heightened or perhaps even countered by
moral considerations claiming a different origin and a higher sanction.
Such aims are explicit in colleges with strong religious affiliations. They
are at least implicit in liberal arts colleges, serving a secularized or
religiously heterogeneous community, which sought, in the spirit of
Matthew Arnold, to put "culture"—that is, some form of the classical
tradition—or, later, some "progressive" form of "humanism" in the
place of religion as an instrument of moral formation.

None of these schools, it must be said, excelled in the training of engineers.[8] If engineers were inclined to think that their activity simply justified itself, many of those who aspired to guide the spirit to higher things apparently felt that engineers, as such, were beyond salvation. This divorce is, I think, symptomatic of a cultural disintegration for which the "separation of fact and value" and the emergence of "two cultures" are but inadequate buzzwords.

In fact, values, though often unexamined, are never absent from educational programs however sober and pragmatic such programs are thought to be. The land grant colleges, for instance, were meant to advance "agriculture, animal husbandry, and the mechanical arts." But they were also charged with advancing democracy, not only by means of the social advancement of their alumni, but also by upholding it as an ideal, as a value. The same can be said of patriotism, a particularly vigorous (and practical) form of which was encouraged by reserve officer training, compulsory for land grant college students. ROTC, no doubt, offers various advantages, but it is neither "value free" nor does it fit naturally in the disinterested pursuit of the truth.

Values, however, seem to the nineteenth-century engineer or engineering enthusiast, not so much juxtaposed as borne out and revealed by facts. The supposed mumbo jumbo of mere talkers can be put aside before the tangible evidence at the disposal of doers:

> Now first we stand and understand,
> And sunder false from true.
> And handle boldly with the hand,
> And see and shape and do.[9]

Putting one's shoulder to the Great Wheel of Progress makes of a man's competence a virtue. Inserted in the great project of bettering the condition of mankind, being useful, is the same as being good. Fulfilling one's appointed task is the same as doing one's duty. The soldier's duty is to his country. The engineer's is even broader: he serves humanity. "Theirs not to reason why."

Many thinkers and educationists have taken a bold stand against the primacy of utility or, in the spirit of Cardinal Newman, proclaimed that liberal studies are, in fact, more useful than any practical training, since knowledge and understanding are always useful. But in its generality such a statement fails to carry conviction. It fails especially to persuade students preparing for profitable careers as it fails to convince their prospective employers. It is, no doubt, right to denounce both industry's point of view, which reduces the university to a delivery system producing employable people—a human resources development mechanism—and the point of view of the students and their parents, which treats it as a vehicle of social aspirations. While the university must be more, much more, it must also be those things—a delivery system and a vehicle of social mobility—or it will be nothing. Whatever else an education is for, it must enable people to make a living, and to the extent that it requires efforts and sacrifices, a better living than they would have without it.

William Barton Rogers, who founded MIT as an alternative to Harvard for the express purpose of training people for business and industry, described the then-new institution's goals in the following terms:

> The education we seek to provide, although eminently practical in its aims, has no affinity with that instruction in mere empirical routine which has sometimes been vaunted as the proper education for those who are to engage in industries. We believe, on the contrary, that the most truly practical education, even in an industrial point of view, is one founded on a thorough knowledge of scientific laws and principles, and one which unites with habits of close observation and exact reasoning, a large general cultivation.[10]

Despite the difference in tone and the reversal of priorities, enlightened practicality taking the place of the universal utility of liberal learning, Newman, I believe, would have had no quarrel with this statement.

3

Second Thoughts: The Needs of Advanced Industrial Societies

It has become customary to decry the careerism of today's students, the lack of "idealism" of the "me generation." There is nothing new, however, about parental aspirations or the ambitions of the young themselves. Already in the twenties, Alfred North Whitehead wrote,

> It was my misfortune to listen (as a member of Royal Commissions on education) to much ineffectual wailing from witnesses on the mercenary tendencies of modern parents. I do not believe that the modern parent of any class is more mercenary than his predecessors. When classics was the road to advancement, classics was the popular subject for study. Opportunity has now shifted its focus . . . was it not Aristotle who said that a good income was a desirable adjunct to an intellectual life?[1]

There is nothing intrinsically dishonorable about wanting to get ahead in life and in any case, allowing for the odd saint, most people do and will continue to act in a manner that they believe is conducive to their material and social advancement. High motives can only operate in conjunction with strong ones, not directly against them. This is not to say that the currents of selfishness and greed should be allowed to sweep everything before them. The free and unguided play of private vice does not, alas, lead straight to public benefit. Nor does the technicist dream of channeling this rush into a kind of turbine to harness its power lead to unambiguously salutary results. Even where it is successful, it produces a power equally capable of good or evil, lacking an intrinsic guiding principle. Civilized human endeavor should perhaps be better seen in the image of a sailboat: fragile but capable of steering a course, not by defying the winds, which would be futile, but by using them. "Nature to be commanded must be obeyed."[2]

There is a place in every civilized society for a genuine ivory tower: a place where intellectual activity serves no other purpose than understanding, with no practical considerations whatever; a place where Japanese calligraphy is studied for its beauty and the revolutions of the stars for the contemplative joy of observing them and not, say, in order to figure out which one of them can serve as a garbage dump in the year 2050. Having said that and granting that a society without such a social space will be barbarous, it needs also be said that such a society need not be dysfunctional. In any particular society, the purely contemplative sphere may be publicly acclaimed or quietly tucked away and, in any event, will rarely exist in perfect isolation from other intellectual interests. It will, in any case, constitute but a small part of the social work and even of the intellectual work performed in any human community. It may constitute the decisive margin by which any given society retains its mental health, but it will be marginal nonetheless. But in any society, the educational system as a whole must and will have functional links to the society's structure and dynamics.

These links are especially clear in industrial societies. The mode of organization of advanced industrial—some would say "post-industrial"[3]—society is predicated on mobility, homogeneity, and growth, and the educational system is geared to bring this about.[4] How this link is perceived in America can be illustrated by an example: In 1951 MIT started a School of Industrial Management. A small committee of distinguished CEO's was brought together to advise the Institute in setting up this new program. The views of this committee are now, forty years later, widely shared by business leaders, though sadly not yet by the mid-level executives who actually do the hiring in most companies.[5] Earl Cheit gives a succinct account of the committee's recommendations:

> They agreed that students should not be taught how to run a company. They thought there was little likelihood that this could be done in any case, and even less chance of doing it in school. . . . The company presidents urged three areas of study: Because significant changes would occur during his working life, the student first would need to know and understand those changes in the context of history in order to be effective in a business career.
>
> Second, . . . students should know how to communicate, because to write and speak effectively are essential leadership skills. Finally . . . the students . . . should be taught something about how human beings behave and why they do what they do. In fact, they agreed that this should be the core of any management program.[6]

How can we explain the fact that but three generations after Leland Stanford, people occupying equivalent positions in American industry seem to demand of university graduates the very qualities that he rejected as useless? Expertise in this or that applied field takes second place after a general sense of the ways of the world. What is wanted are not taciturn doers but eloquent speakers and lucid writers. The perceived need for skill in dealing with things has given way to a desire for a measure of prudence and understanding in human affairs. Are we to suppose that these successful men were moved by vanity to indulge in ideological anachronism? Should we assume that, having arrived themselves, they were led to express atavistic yearnings for the "gentlemanly" accomplishments that used to be the preserve of people whose liberal education befitted their "good stock"? It does not seem likely. These were hard-nosed businessmen, as committed to efficiency and rationality as any man. As advisers to MIT they were, in any case, concerned not with their sons and daughters as such, but with the best preparation of their future employees and eventual colleagues.

The truth is, in a highly developed industrial society, fewer and fewer people need to handle things, and more and more need to manipulate meanings. Growing productivity requires not only an ever-higher degree of differentiation in the division of labor, not only, that is, an ever-greater number of more refined specialisms, but also rapid transformations in the pattern of employment. The position of any job, relative to the system as a whole, is liable to change, as are the persons, or the kinds of persons, holding particular jobs or particular types of jobs. Job specifications themselves change rapidly. By some indicators it would appear, for instance, that about every five years some 50 percent of all industrially pertinent engineering specializations become obsolete.

Unlike the circumscribed career patterns in agrarian, and even in early industrial societies, people can no longer expect to hold the same occupational role all their lives. Much less can they expect, for better or for worse, to hand it down to their children. Advanced industrial society requires an unprecedented degree of mobility. At the same time, occupational roles are ever-more important in determining people's identity and self-respect. It means, on the one hand, a world of "careers open to talent." This was perceived as a functional requirement as early as 1910.

> "The career open to talent" is no longer a matter of abstract humanitarian theory . . . for the great industrial communities of the modern world it is a cogent practical necessity imposed by the fierce international competition which prevails in the arts and industries of life. The notion that is not to fail in the struggle for commercial success, with all that this implies for national life and civilization, must needs see that its industries are fed with a constant supply of workers adequately equipped in respect to both general intelligence and technical training.[7]

By the same token, it means the obsolescence of highly specialized skills, developed over a long time, often a lifetime or even generations. It is an often painful transition, as we can currently see in the Rust Belt, for example. In higher strata as well, maintenance of social status requires a high degree of mobility. It will no longer do to join dad at the firm, learn the ropes at his side, and then inherit the business. To be maintained, advantages must be translated—through education—into versatile skills applicable to the kaleidoscopic changes of corporate organization. This is one reason for the progressive disappearance of the gentleman's C.

Change in the pattern of the division of labor has become the one permanent feature of the social order. The paradoxical truth is that highly specialized industrial society must rest on a broad basis of generic, standardized, nonspecialized knowledge and training. The return to the fundamental need for a general education, only now on a much broader basis, is not the vain attempt to reintroduce exclusionary devices, but is, on the contrary, the result of the egalitarian pressures of industrial development.

Industrial societies can no longer rely on informal, personal transmission of skills, father to son, master to apprentice, etc. They must instead rely on formalized patterns of learning, leading to a more or less reliable system of certification. As the requisite level of accomplishment and, not least, the pressure of ever-greater numbers of certified competitors within this broadly homogeneous, mobile job market increases, so does the level of education pursued.[8] (The skyrocketing price of university education is, no doubt, in great part due to the great social and economic value it has acquired.) By an extension of the same logic, except at the very highest level of creative activity, an advanced industrial society can no longer rely on specialists to activate the stock of cumulative technical and scientific knowledge on which it relies; it needs instead to move people around as need arises—people prepared to face new and unexpected aspects of this common stock of knowledge and its applications. The preparation of people suited to this kind of society will then have to consist less in a specialized expertise and more in a trained capacity to learn, a language, as it were, that allows them to become conversant with the world they inhabit.

4

Literacy and Democracy

We have so far treated nontechnical university education and the MIT committee's recommendations from a strictly functional point of view— insofar, that is, as it serves to create optimally employable and upwardly mobile people. But it is easy to mistake this functional congruence with the requirements of industrialism for good citizenship. Good citizenship has a qualitative dimension, which is different from the leveling effect of the mobile occupational structures needed and brought about by industrial development. Whether one salutes the abolition of traditional barriers as the triumphant march of equality, rationality, and justice or deplores it as the passing and flattening out of a more picturesque world, it is unquestionably underwritten by the dynamism of industrial society itself. An undeniable egalitarian impetus affects higher education but encompasses, of course, the entire educational system. One should be wary, however, of identifying this egalitarianism with democracy, if by democracy we mean not only equality of rank, but also the structures of ordered liberty. The paradox of universal *compulsory* education, which suggests that people have to be *forced* to enjoy what is taken to be an elementary democratic *entitlement*, should make us sit up and think.

The president of the Andrew Mellon Foundation is one of many conscientious voices expressing concern about the state of literacy in America:

> In spite of the fact that some improvements are now underway, and that a backward glance reveals evidence of genuine progress over the course of the last several decades, it is nonetheless the case that the demands and expectations of our society are changing rapidly, and are in fact currently outpacing the capacity of our educational system to respond. More situations in ordinary life—and certainly in the world of employment— require individuals to read instructions, directions, correspondence, and other forms of communication than ever before. In addition, we routinely expect individuals to take messages and summarize them in writing, or to cope with train and bus timetables or checkbook and bank

statements, income tax forms, safety instructions and manuals, and a host of other materials that are part of modern life and that were far less pervasive in earlier eras.[1]

All the skills enumerated are undoubtedly valuable, indeed necessary to the well-being of society and of each of its members. But they are all functional skills, essential to the efficient function of a bureaucratically administered technological world, as necessary in a democracy as in the bleakest tyranny.

Industrialism, it seems, must be egalitarian. It is far from clear that it needs to be liberal. Members of illiterate nomadic tribes may well enjoy a greater degree of freedom and have more of a say in their common affairs than highly literate subjects of a bureaucratic regime. The Oxford anthropologist and philosopher Ernest Gellner, points out the paradox:

> The ideal of universal literacy and the right to education is a well-known part of the pantheon of modern values. It is spoken of with respect by statesmen and politicians and enshrined in declarations of rights, constitutions, party programmes and so forth. So far, nothing unusual. The same is true of representative and accountable government, free elections, an independent judiciary, freedom of speech and assembly, and so on. Many or most of these admirable values are often and systematically ignored in many parts of the world, without anyone batting an eyelid. Very often, it is safe to consider these phrases as simple verbiage. . . . What is so curious, and highly significant about the principle of universal and centrally guaranteed education, is that it is an ideal more honoured in the observance than in the breach. In this, it is virtually unique among modern ideals.[2]

We are accustomed to consider the drive toward homogeneity, as the condition of mobility, almost entirely in terms of entitlement and advancement. We are less inclined to look at it in terms of obligation and compulsion. The question whether, for example, women should be allowed to fight, to "assume," as the jargon has it, "a combat role" in the armed forces has a flip side. In a coherent, homogeneous world, on what logical basis can women be exempted from military service? It is not to play down the vigor and moral courage of groups struggling for equal status to say that their success and, in large part, their motivation is due to the equalizing dynamism of industrial society. In traditional societies, people are marked by relatively stable patterns of distinctive and unequal identity, legitimized by time and custom. But in a society predicated on growth and mobility, distinctions and inequalities must be transformed into a homogeneous continuum within which it is possible to move. Gellner writes,

Modern society is not mobile because it is egalitarian, it is egalitarian be-cause it is mobile. Stratification and inequality do exist, and sometimes in extreme form; nevertheless they have a muted and discreet quality, at-tenuated by a kind of gradualness of the distinctions of wealth and standing, a lack of social distance and a convergence of lifestyle, a kind of statistical or probabilistic quality of the differences (as opposed to the rigid, absolutized, chasm-like differences typical of agrarian society) and by the illusion or reality of social mobility. That illusion is essential, and it cannot persist without at least a measure of reality.[3]

5

Technology and Freedom

Whatever its possible drawbacks, in today's world the industrial economy with its leveling imperatives is not an option that can be chosen or rejected. Humanity is irreversibly committed to it. The survival of the world's population and what measure of civil peace can be achieved depends on it.[1]

Industrial society depends on sustained and perpetual material and cognitive growth. If one were to reverse the process, supposing that were possible, half the people in the world would starve, and the other half would be at each others' throats. We cannot predict all the consequences of administrative-industrial development. No doubt there is cause for concern, not least ecological concern, just as there is cause for hope. But there is no turning back. We cannot sail straight into the wind. We can only tack as adroitly as we can. But this requires more than the possession of a cumulative body of knowledge made available by specialized experts. It requires, like citizenship, a qualitative capacity of judgment and good sense.[2]

It is tempting, on the other hand, to identify the apparently most efficient social mechanism for economic growth with the most desirable political arrangements. A lot of people took cheer from the long lines waiting to get a McMuffin just around the corner from the Kremlin. As long as democracy, economic rationality, and technological growth are thought to be naturally linked, the ingenuous optimism of our nineteenth-century populist utilitarianism can continue unabated, and we can congratulate ourselves that fast food, borne on the wings of free trade, has made an impeccably democratic addition to Russian cuisine. The president of the National Academy of Engineering, Robert M. White, writes, with cheerful confidence, that

> Technology in its myriad forms, from surveillance satellites to instant communication, has helped to keep the peace and to publicize the moral bankruptcy of oppression. . . .
>
> In effect, technology is the foundation of an open society. Citizens on either side of the Iron Curtain could not forever remain ignorant of the

fortunes of their neighbors, nor could the world escape the terrible images of the massacre in Tienanmen Square. Where technology has failed to penetrate, as in Burma, Albania and Tibet, repression continues unremarked, but unabated.

If technology has become a catalyst for peaceful change, then it may also become a mechanism for its permanent adoption. Technology has become the wellspring of global economic prosperity; the desire for economic growth has fueled the desire for political change. Success in invigorating the mothballed economic system of Eastern Europe will depend on technology. By encouraging the diffusion of technology around the globe, Western nations can prevent these emerging democracies from slipping back into the twilight of Marxism.[3]

There is, no doubt, a lot of truth in this statement, but there is also a great deal of wishful thinking and selective vision. It is comforting to believe in a mechanism in which the rationality of greed will eventually master the irrationalities of all other human passions, and the end result, if not the "end of history," will be a world, peaceful and affluent, if somewhat bland and monotonous.[4] In order to believe in a functional link between technology, on the one hand, and desirable social forms, democracy and peace, on the other, we must, for example, stress technology's contribution to providing information to and for the benefit of citizens rather than, say, its strength in gathering information on them; its capacity to spread news rather than propaganda; to inform rather than flatter or titillate the public. We must believe that the penetration of technology into Abyssinia, to take a sufficiently remote example, in the form of Italian flame throwers and lethal gas is simply a thing of the past and that the unbelievable technological-organizational impetus that made Hitler's "final solution" possible was a historical aberration that will be ironed out by the long-term operation of technological growth and the human attitudes it requires and engineers.

The optimistic confidence that technological development will inevitably result in universal peace and prosperity rests, I think, on two presuppositions. The first is the notion that all human predicaments can be transformed into problems and thus become, in principle, capable of resolution by deliberate, conscious action. This involves the transfer of a manner of rationality proper to technical thinking to the entire field of meaningful, value-laden human engagements. Technological endeavor is, then, no longer inscribed in a more comprehensive (and, naturally, more elusive) world of value but becomes itself the touchstone of value by collapsing the desirable into the feasible. In this perspective technology is not merely a power, but, as it was for Tennyson, a virtue.

The second presupposition is that this power for the good develops according to an inner logic, shaping events in such a way that it furthers its own realization. What is desirable and feasible is also inevitable. The vision of a technical fix for the political problems of humanity is heightened when it is viewed as self-realizing. A president of the U.S. with a solid reputation of being sensible, Harry Truman, was not immune to the siren song of the Great Technical Fix, its philanthropic promise made possible by the providential unfolding of man's technical power. One day, he pulled a yellowed piece of paper from his pocket and read to an astonished journalist some lines he had copied from Tennyson's "Locksley Hall":[5]

> For I dipt into the future, far as human eye could see.
> Saw the vision of the world, and all the wonder that would be:
> . . . .
> Heard the Heavens fill with shouting and there rained a ghastly dew
> From the nations' airy navies grappling in the central blue;
>
> Far along the world-wide whisper, of the south wind rushing warm
> With the standards of the peoples plunging through the thunderstorm
>
> Till the war drums throbbed no longer and the battle flags were furled
> In the Parliament of Man, the Federation of the World.

A week later Truman ordered the nuclear attack on Hiroshima, and soon after he was in San Francisco for the founding of the United Nations. What is at issue here is not the wisdom or humanity of these acts of state, but rather the hope for an *ultimate* answer to the great problems afflicting mankind resulting from the dynamics of technological development.

We face two contradictions. The first lies in the trust or hope that a permanent, stable condition of peace, democracy, or the "end of history," can result from a process that is essentially dynamic, predicated on change and growth without limit. From a purely technical point of view, this contradictory aspiration gives rise to the fallacy of the last move as presented for instance by some of the more sweeping (and popular) claims in favor of the Strategic Defense Initiative (SDI). The nature of technology is such that there is no device for which a counter cannot be devised. Leaving the question of armaments aside, it is often argued, as we saw, that mechanisms operating in the economic sphere will inevitably lead to freedom, not because freedom is desirable in itself but because it is a necessary condition of an efficient economy.

That there is some truth to that recent events make difficult to doubt. But this leads to the second contradiction: freedom should spring from necessity.

The events of 1989 were truly wonderful. Do they permit us, however, to congratulate ourselves and rest assured that the blessings of liberty are secured for us and our posterity—allowing for occasional delays and reversals for the rest of mankind—because they seem best suited to deliver the goods?

That the imperatives of technological civilization are felt everywhere is, I should think, undeniable. The way in which they play out, however, the manner in which particular polities emerge and evolve, the way in which particular lives are conducted show variations irreducible to the determination of industrial rationality. The revival of human agency in the context of emerging or reemerging civil societies in Eastern Europe, often—too often—coupled with violence, seems to indicate that other forces are at play.

Given favorable circumstances, the Czechs chose to live freely because they wanted to be free, not just because they wanted full store shelves. Others with similar opportunities seem to have chosen differently. What we witnessed in 1989 was not the "end of history"; on the contrary, it was the defrosting of civil society frozen by totalitarianism. The widespread violence that came with the decline of the Soviet Empire is also sad but certain evidence of human agency. It is far from self-evident that the final result will be liberal democracy, peace, and prosperity. Liberty means the ability to choose between good and evil, and with liberty comes the need for a liberal education. We cannot entrust freedom to mechanisms, be it of machines—satellites, computers, faxes—be it of the market.

6

Efficiency vs. the Love of One's Own

In an editorial entitled "Engineering and the Discipline of the Marketplace,"[1] John F. Welch, Jr., chairman of the National Academy of Engineering (NAE), discusses the importance of engineering and the role of the NAE in restoring America's competitive edge in the global marketplace. He notes that other countries have adopted industrial and trade policies that have led them to a measure of success such as to compel the U.S. to think twice. Nevertheless, he writes,

> Whereas other nations have done quite well with structured, orchestrated, and subsidized industrial strategies, our culture, our history, our national personality would not and should not encourage that approach.[2]

The NAE chairman is, of course, looking for efficient solutions. But he is looking for satisfactory solutions within a framework circumscribed by cultural considerations that are cherished regardless of their relative capacity to deliver the goods. His attachment to the American way of doing things seems to transcend the stubborn fact that, at least for the moment, in some important areas, it is no longer the most efficient way. Economic and sociocultural values are not automatically congruent. For the argument advanced by Welch to be persuasive, his own attachment and that of his readers to the "national personality" must have a hold that goes beyond morally inert utility.

That this manner of attachment makes itself felt in what is certainly meant as a levelheaded argument shows that it is indeed such attachments, all calculations aside, that make us this rather than that, heirs to this rather than that history, brought up to value this rather than that way of doing things. There is more to this than the means-ends rationality of know-how. Even when we become wisely self-critical, we can only adapt and rearrange what we already are. We cannot invent ourselves out of nothing. What is involved is something else than adding yet another item of knowledge to our stock. Like judgment and common sense, a sense of identity is personal. Unlike scientific and technical knowledge, it can be neither cumulated nor divided into discrete fields of expertise.

We are reminded that human personalities do not mature against a background of abstract rationality but within the context of a way of life, which is always a particular way of life. One does not learn to speak by learning "language," but by learning a particular language. The American way is not everyone's way, and those who are attached to it are those who are formed by it. It is not really a matter of choice, although a tradition of absorbing immigrants, and the voluntarist rhetoric of American culture may sometimes lead one to think so. We are not really attached to our mothers because, as we tell them and maybe tell ourselves, they are the best in the world. We do not choose a culture because it offers the best product for the price. It is, rather, the vast complex of institutions and mores, of shared activities and modes of conduct that constitutes the matrix in terms of which we value some things over others. The structure of a language does not, of course, determine the content of the utterances made in that language, and, correspondingly, a way of life, in terms of which a pattern of conduct is meaningful, does not determine such conduct. But the relative freedom of movement within a culture, and indeed the possibility of transcending it, will be in the measure of one's mastery of it.

7

Cultural Literacy

It is clear that formal schooling can only be a part, in most cases but a small part, in the transmission of culture. Too many things are unspoken, built into the manner of doing things, to be the objects of explicit teachings. Those who convey cultural lessons embody them rather than know them as things that they can separate from themselves. Factual information, precepts, and admonitions are important, of course. But one acquires one's culture principally by living with people, by living as they do.

The more articulate modes of culture have traditionally been the possession of the few. Democracy and the egalitarian pressures of industrial society lead to demands that "high" culture be made available to all. Robert M. Hutchins, for instance, wrote a sentence of programmatic importance for his efforts: "The best education for the best is the best education for all." It is a sentence expressing impeccable democratic sentiment linked to an unwavering dedication to excellence. The truth is that the same educational offerings presented by the very same teachers will not have the same effect on students who come to their studies with different horizons. All teaching presupposes a preexistent body of knowledge and a command of language such as to make what is said much more suggestive and intelligible to those who, in a sense, already know.[1] The problem, which probably has no perfect solution, is how to do one's best by those whose access to general culture is almost entirely dependent on formal schooling, and still provide something like the "best education." There are those who would reject such an effort out of hand, arguing that educational values are merely functions of social values, that the very notion of high culture is "elitist" and that instead of trying to make it accessible to all, one should affirm popular culture or the patchwork of popular cultures, however understood, as they stand, all intellectual considerations being subjugated to questions of power.[2]

What formal schooling can provide will never be the kind of unforced culture that comes from frequenting cultured, and not just learned, people (what the French call *culture libre*). There is no getting away from the fact that students benefit differentially depending on their background, and backgrounds cannot be supplied to order. The importance of supportive families for scholastic achievement has been demonstrated repeatedly. The comparative success of immigrant groups from East and Southeast Asia seems to bear it out, and the Japanese mother has become proverbial. Studies by Senator Daniel Patrick Moynihan and others have shown that the amount of money per student spent in various states and school districts makes little difference in terms of academic results when measured against the family life (not primarily the socioeconomic position of the family!) of the students.[3] Spending money on schools can do no harm, but the roots of the problem are deeper and much more difficult to deal with.

In an optimistic "can do" society, such facts and their sobering implications are not easily admitted, and yet the problems created by the exclusion of significant sections of the population from the functional "high" culture are more urgent than ever. However urgent or unfortunate such disparities may be, they do not appear problematic from the point of view of social cohesion as long as elites, defined precisely by the possession of the functional high culture, give the tone and are deferred to, however informally. When, however, secondary and in the course of events, postsecondary education (with the entitlements it is considered to confer) spreads to ever-greater numbers, tendentially to the entire pertinent age groups, and is coupled with expectations of entitlement and advancement, the disparities are acutely felt and are experienced as scandalous. Since for a number of reasons little can be done or, at any rate, little is done about the direct social causes of such disparities, the problem devolves on the one ever-available instrument of social thinking, or, better, the convenient ersatz social policy offered by the schools. The schools are then blamed for not doing what is, in fact, beyond their power.

We should be careful not to blame the schools, even as we express our concern about the state they are in. Schools have been saddled with any number of problems society did not wish to confront in a more immediate fashion, from racial integration to drug and sex counseling, from social promotion of the disadvantaged to special care of the disabled.

Overburdened as they are, they cannot help but fall short of expectations in the ever-proliferating social tasks they have been made to perform and, in so doing, also drag down the quality of their proper task, namely, schooling. Society, having dumped its problems on the schools, can then make a scapegoat of the schools for not fixing them.

This is the situation that E. D. Hirsch and his project of "Cultural Literacy" takes seriously.[4] Making every man a philosopher may not be possible or even desirable, and culture in T. S. Eliot's sense may well be predicated on class.[5] Hirsch's crucial argument, however, both democratic and humane, is that the family (where it exists at all) and other informal structures often fail to provide access to the shared attitudes, conventions, and civilizational points of reference that constitute the medium of nationwide communication and that where this is so, something should be done about it. His approach, whatever its drawbacks, clearly faces the problem of the cultural conditions of the ability to learn.

Culture, or at least functional "high" culture amounts, according to Hirsch, to a body of information: "Our children," he writes, "can learn this information by being taught it." There is, admittedly, something thin about such a notion of culture. Learning the elements of "cultural literacy" from the list in the back of Hirsch's book, from "absolute zero" to "zeitgeist" is not unlike trying to learn good manners from an etiquette book. But Hirsch himself does not pretend that "cultural literacy" is all there is to education, and promoting it is certainly better than sitting on one's hands and letting the devil take the hindmost.

It is the business of education, according to Hirsch, to provide a common world of reference or, as he puts it, to make everyone culturally literate, that is to make everyone conversant with what is, in fact, the dominant "high" culture of the U.S. The reason for doing this, he believes, is not the normative content of this high culture, but simply the fact that it is the common world of reference, the indispensable medium of effective communication and mobility, and therefore also the vehicle of social advancement: "The inherent conservatism of literacy leads to a subtle but unavoidable paradox: the goals of political liberalism require educational conservatism. We make social and economic programs *only* by teaching myths and facts that are predominantly traditional."[6]

One of the great merits of the book *Cultural Literacy* is that it has forcefully put before the public the idea that we can only understand things in terms of things already understood, that we can only communicate with others in terms that we share with them. Linked to that is Hirsch's reasoned opposition to the sentimental excesses of "student-centered" learning, to the idea, that is, that one can learn to learn without actually learning anything. Hence the need, articulated by

Hirsch, for a common world of reference or cultural literacy. It follows that we are not free to choose any frame of reference. In the absence of a given frame, in what terms could any rational preference be expressed? The framework must be, argues Hirsch, that of the national functional high culture. Anyone who does not achieve cultural literacy is condemned to remain marginal.[7]

8

Of Content and Form in Teaching

The cultural vacuum created by several generations of "content-neu-tral" education is truly deplorable. Progressive reformers like Dewey, taking their cue, no doubt, from their own extraordinary teaching skills and intellectual vivacity, designed a pedagogic method that needs to live on its wits. A routine, like old-fashioned teaching, designed to be a routine, is no worse when it is institutionalized. Progressive education institutionalized turns to clay. The common teacher, dutiful and hard-working, gifted even, but lacking the intellectual horizon and the liveli-ness of a Dewey, has nothing to fall back on, and neither does his student. Behind the prepositions that command the dative, there is always Caesar or Virgil, and a student may catch fire despite, if not because of, teachers. Behind "fundamental processes," "cognitional skills," and "critical thinking," taught by a teacher who has himself been taught nothing but "education," there is nothing. Hence the de-sire, expressed by Hirsch and others, to return to substantive learning.

The traditional teacher is authoritative when one is fortunate and authoritarian when one is not. But, unlike the progressive teacher, he does not pretend to be a "facilitator," one "enabling the student to think for himself" except indirectly, by initiating the student to a world of reference. The student may be bored and perhaps browbeaten by the traditional teacher, but he is not misled. For all the "softness" of his method and, alas, also of his subject matter, the progressive teacher remains a figure of authority, and the student, with an eye to his grade, is no less eager to come up with "the right answer," that is the answer he believes will please teacher.

What is at issue is not the authority of teachers, which has its proper, inevitable, and salutary place. It is, rather, the idea that intellectual and social skills, the capacity to make one's way in the economic, political, cultural setting of one's country, could be inculcated directly, as though it were a vocational aptitude that could be picked up by the study of the appropriate brief manual. Explicitly utilitarian in its outlook, progres-sive education sought to transfer the manner characteristic of late nineteenth-century technical training to general education.[1] One can see why it would have seemed attractive to well-meaning democratic educators. In its content-neutral emphasis on procedures it seemed evenhanded with regard to students with different levels and, in a country of immigrants, culturally different kinds of preparation. In its rationalist optimism it sought to cut through the tangle of intricate, potentially divisive, historical accretions composing American culture. In its pragmatism it sought to effect immediate outcomes in terms of professional competence, citizenship, and mobility, much as a drill sergeant seeks to form a recruit. The discarding of history in favor of "social studies" is symptomatic of this flight forward from the contingencies of cultural reality to the dream of abstract empowering skills.[2]

We have seen that technical education itself can no longer be properly conducted with a view to immediate vocational utility but that a more roundabout way yields better long-term results. It should be even more evident that the general cultivation of a human being, her political and cultural education, cannot be effected directly. Hirsch's efforts, though better than inaction, are, I believe, subject to the same rationalist fallacy.

One can conceive of a general education that avoids the deceptive shortcuts of progressive social engineering by making sure that it is grounded in substantive learning. One can, at the same time, guard against the dangers of traditionalist pedantry by means of another indirection: small discussion classes that succeed in becoming genuine communities of learning. The very form and civility of conversation, where that can be achieved, constitute a cultural accomplishment and a vehicle of learning more valuable than any pragmatic outcome, social or intellectual, that direct didactic efforts could hope to accomplish. In civilized conversation about matters that make up the intellectual landscape we inhabit, the form and content of a liberal education come together. Such an education is, of course, not teacher-proof, and small classes are expensive. High schools and colleges will not be easily persuaded to adopt such an approach, but one of its chief attractions is that it is, in principle, open to all. A few successful examples would provide food for thought.

Part 2

The American Way
in Liberal Education

9

The Tower of Babel

One need not fully share Hirsch's high-minded optimism to admire his intentions. His (at least preliminary) agnosticism with regard to the intrinsic value of the content of American literate culture, as opposed to its functional utility, is a prudent refusal to engage in an ideological argument when practical, pragmatic arguments promise a better, broader basis of agreement. His emphasis is, however, altogether on the instrumental rather than on what may be called the properly liberal side of culture:

> Why is literacy so important in the modern world? Some of the reasons, like the need to fill out forms to get a good job, are so obvious that they needn't be discussed. But the chief reason is broader. The complex undertakings of modern life depend on the cooperation of many people with different specialties in different places. When communications fail, so do the undertakings. (That is the moral of the story of the Tower of Babel.) The function of the national literacy is to foster effective nationwide communications. . . . Mature literacy alone enables the tower to be built, the business to be well managed, and the airplane to fly without crashing.[1]

Well, so much for the sin of pride, for a sense of human finitude, and for the notion that a wise Providence may have wanted the world peopled by several peoples of various tongues, rather than by the tyrant Nimrod's monolingual tribe.[2] What, one might ask, is the Tower of Babel for?

The evocation of the Tower of Babel raises two questions. The first is about the scope and the degree of cultural unity necessary for human beings to accomplish their appointed tasks. The second is about the apparent inability of modern science and technology, perhaps of modern society itself, as marked by modern science, to determine the meaning of its own undertakings.

Let me begin with the question of scope. We have seen how, even in the face of the pressures of economic rationality, a national way of life asserts itself. It appeared that the powerful equalizing force of modern industrial society allowed for a considerable degree of variation and that technically and economically competent—or perhaps one should say competitive—societies were nonetheless capable of different, historically and culturally distinct articulations of their respective ways of life. France, Germany, and Japan, for example, though all unmistakably modern, are also unmistakably French, German, and Japanese, respectively. It follows that, although one can meaningfully speak of degrees of modernity or modernization, civilizations do not represent stages on a unilineal continuum, rather they are marked by distinct, properly cultural characteristics. Civilization does not run on rails, each culture-train passing through the same stations, some rushing ahead, and others lagging behind. Each culture, at any given time, results from a great number of things that come together, for better or for worse, not the least of which, of course, is the ineluctable process of technological development.

One uncomfortable conclusion is that cultures are remarkably elusive entities. They are difficult to delimit with any precision. The decisive characteristics that set them apart—demographic, linguistic, social, historical, political, psychological, etc.—are uncertain and controversial. The difficulty of delimiting a culture toward the outside is compounded by the question of the requisite degree of inner unity and homogeneity. We saw that Hirsch's argument hinges on the need for a broadly if not universally shared functional "high" culture as an essential bond of cohesion, a medium of communication and mobility. If modern civilization allows for some international variation, it seems, nonetheless, to require a certain degree of homogeneity *within* any one culture, sufficiently defined for practical purposes—at least for the U.S.—by the borders of the national territory.

A national community, though its government derive its just powers from the consent of the governed, is not a voluntary association resulting from a utilitarian calculus of its several members. It is held together by multiple, institutional, symbolic, and historical bonds. It is natural to develop loyalty to what one recognizes as one's own both because it is one's own and because one experiences its worth as attached to one's own feeling of self-worth. The constitution and cultivation of a national identity can, however, go beyond that. From being the major custodian of cultural identity the nation can become the object of a cult.

It is one thing, I think, to note the existence of a religious quality to social cohesion and to study its workings.[3] It is quite another to advocate national integration in the mode of a religious observance. It is precisely in this regard that E. D. Hirsch departs from his "value-free" functionalist view of American culture. He observes, correctly I think, that "few of us accept the extreme and impractical idea that our unity can be a purely legal umbrella, which formally contains but does not integrate our diversity."[4] Besides the English language and the law, Hirsch points out, American society is held together by an ethos. Interestingly, he does not see civil religion as a ritual exaltation of an underlying ethos but, inversely, the ethos as a function of civil religion.[5] In the beginning is not a practice, but a faith. Integration is envisaged in the image of profession and conversion. This civil religion, which "lends coherence to the larger American public culture and is the basic source [sic] of American values," Hirsch unhesitatingly embraces and affirms.[6] The Constitution, he tells us, is its Bible. As such, it is revered. Its author, the Nation as the Sovereign People, retains, however, the power and the right to change it. We are reminded of the Hebrew Covenant, except that its two poles, the Author of the Law and the People Receiving the Law, are collapsed into one. The Nation as the Sovereign People is divine, or at least the proper object of a religious cult, and it achieves its own coherence by worshiping itself. Hirsch, who refers to Gellner in the "functional" part of his analysis, does not quote him in this context: "Durkheim taught that in religious worship society adores its own camouflaged image. In a nationalist age, societies worship themselves brazenly, spurning the camouflage."[7] Public education would then have to be a catechism in civil theology. This is not, I think, a liberal task. What is needed is, rather, a respectful, but not unthinking, familiarity with the country's institutional and symbolic articulation.[8]

10

E Pluribus Unum?

That all men are created equal is unquestionably one of the propositions central to the symbolic order of the United States. It is, naturally, not perfectly reflected in the actual conduct of Americans, but it does create aspirations and raise expectations that inform American life. Not only do we find a frequently reiterated ideological commitment to equality but also, in actual practice, an absence of distinctions of rank, an informality and lack of deference that foreign visitors from Tocqueville to D. H. Lawrence have not failed to notice. This democracy of manners agrees, one is tempted to say providentially, with the egalitarian dynamism of modern industrialism. Whatever the causal nexus between ideological outlook and functional structure might be, there is no question that the leveling effect of this general process meets, on the whole, with widespread social approval.

What is intolerable by the standards of the American way of life is pretending to differences of kind, viewed as tantamount to "putting on airs." Differences of degree, on the other hand, though often resented and certainly present in the actual distribution of material and moral benefits, are tolerated, even welcomed, as long as they are seen to be quantitative, commensurable differences, such as differences in wealth. The disparity between the principle of equality and material inequality is mediated by sporting, that is to say procedural and *formal* requirements such as "equality of opportunity" and a "level playing field."[1]

Beyond the idea of a homogeneous continuum, Americans, for the most part, also value living in a tolerant and diverse society. Whatever the requirements of economic rationality and social mobility, few people—one hopes—are melancholy enough to believe that transforming human beings into interchangeable parts of a huge impersonal social machine is anything but horrible. The life of any human being would be immensely impoverished if it drew all its value from its place as a cog in the machine. A worthwhile human life brings together different attachments, some voluntary and some given. These attachments and the characteristic activities, the joys and pains that go with them, refuse to be neatly packed into each other and ultimately subordinated to one's place in the great machine. They cut different ways. A society in which all have everything in common is poor, and a society in which all are compelled to have everything in common is totalitarian. If, on the one hand, homogeneity is functional, on the other hand, variety is the spice of life. You cannot make a city out of people who are all alike, wrote Aristotle.[2]

The city, which makes the good life possible, requires members different in kind, whose capacities complement each other beyond the conventional understanding of the division of labor. But variety is not equality because one cannot be both different and the same. Aristotle, who was not a democrat, saw no difficulty in this. But Americans, who are democrats, reconcile the principle of equality with the understanding that "it takes all kinds," by means of the notion of individual rights. Here again we have a formal principle mediating what is an apparent substantive contradiction. The principle of equal rights does not mean that preferences and practices covered by these rights are equal, that is the same or equivalent, but that they are treated, in certain significant respects, *as though* they were equal. Equal law for all, to quote the inscription on the front of the Supreme Court, suggests that it is *the law* that is equal with regard to those who stand before it. Equal rights do not engage the content of rights but establish the procedural and constitutional equality of those who hold them. It becomes possible, then, to uphold equality and pluralism at the same time.[3]

In light of this, it would seem to be the business of a general education to orient the student less toward any particular outcomes of public action than to a grasp of the formal conditions of possibility of legitimate action. By this I do not mean simply adequate information about the organs of government and the Constitution itself—though that is sorely lacking—but occasions to develop a sense for the importance of forms, such as due process, the value of which always surpasses the particular outcomes they may produce.

What is involved, yet again, is a necessary and salutary indirection of pedagogical efforts that should aim to establish a maturity of judgment rather than purportedly desirable convictions. Since it is always important to practice what one preaches, it will be of great value to give some intimation of proper procedural forms by example as much as by precept. In this sense the manner of teaching is, perhaps, even more important than the subject matter. To be conversant with the forms of a civilization is to master a style, a way of life.

Members of a good society will not have everything in common, yet, if they had nothing in common there would be no society. In a country of immigrants, the question of a shared culture versus the claims of particularist, historically and culturally constituted modes of identity, is posed in a special way. It is evident that the decisive part of what is shared, and comes to be shared by newcomers, will be in the mode of those already in place. This is especially so, since with notable exceptions, immigrants tend to be drawn from the disadvantaged and culturally less articulate strata of their countries of origin. However strong the impress of the culture of the old country may be in the anthropological sense, intellectual sophistication along with rising in the world must, on the whole, take the form of assimilation. The multiple and successive graftings do, of course, change the nature of the old tree and of the fruit it is liable to produce. Conversely, the sap of the old trunk affects the new growth. The integrative power of America is hard to underestimate.

The functionally integrated, hyphenated American, while retaining vestiges of ethnic identity, is in truth assimilated. An interesting study of Greek-Americans, borne out by my own anecdotal experience, showed that though they themselves thought of themselves as very Greek, relatives visiting from the old country found them thoroughly Americanized.[4] In some respects the pattern of acculturation and individual absorption into "mainstream" culture is all the stronger for being in practice compatible with the subjective assertions of ethnic cultural links, characteristically revived in the third generation. But these vestiges are not nothing. Although the Irish of Ireland are very different from the Irish of Massachusetts, and the Italians of Italy are very different from the Italians of New Jersey, yet there is something recognizably particular about Irish-American or Italian-American communities, offering ascriptive bonds that do not conflict with the tenor of the encompassing general culture, because they are deeply marked by it. What one could call the sociologically Protestant tone of the Roman Church in America is a related phenomenon.

In this spirit, the challenge of diversity consists in socializing into the pattern of advanced industrial society and the forms of the American polity of people whose habits of mind have been otherwise formed. Unlike nativism or racist discrimination, efforts in this direction are fired by the hope, if not the certitude, that such a transformation can be effected regardless of race, culture, or social origin. They are borne by the conviction that such change ought to be effected, both for the benefit of individuals, who are thus enabled to go their own way, and for the benefit of the whole, to which they are empowered to contribute. This integrationist outlook is often accompanied by a benevolence toward and sometimes even a delight in the variety of mores manifested in the private realm. It is possible, however, to underestimate the degree to which traditional mores, taken seriously, inevitably affect public conduct just as, conversely, it is easy to overestimate the degree of cultural uniformity necessary for an orderly modern society to function.

Engineers have been active and open-minded proponents of integrative diversity. This is, no doubt, in part due to the earthy realism and lack of social pretensions characteristic of the engineer. Engineers know that good people, properly trained, can do the job. The technical and organizational rationality that underlies engineering is not, of course, naturally given to all human beings but is itself a cultural product. When Ferdinand de Lesseps introduced wheelbarrows to the building sites of the Suez Canal, the workmen, not knowing what to do with them, put them on their heads. But compared to political culture or literature, for example, the language of engineering and its applications can be most easily divorced from its historical matrix. There are, interestingly enough, distinct *styles* of engineering, and a person trained in one place may be inclined to tunnel through a mountain, whereas one trained in another may prefer to blast through it. But the differences are marginal, and engineering has a universality akin to that of mathematics, because unlike other human endeavors, it engages the detached intelligence, not the identity of its practitioner. It is perhaps no accident that the spectacular success of East Asian students and scholars in the U.S. is largely in those fields that depend least on cultural associations: mathematics, the pure and applied sciences. Engineering attracts and—for the purpose of our present argument, more important—accommodates a larger percentage of foreign-born teachers than any other academic field in America. According to data presented at the 1990 annual national meeting of engineering deans, over half the assistant professors in American schools in engineering were born overseas. The percentage of foreign graduate students, only some of whom will return to their countries of origin, is also correspondingly large.

Engineering executives and engineering educators, for example, who have—at least in America—traditionally attracted "entry level" social strata and who now face a shortage of recruits, are eager to win over women and minority students and are deeply concerned about the elementary and secondary preparation that such students receive. It is not that they want to see the vocabulary of engineering practice enriched by new dialects, the building of, say, recognizably Hispanic differentials or the development of microchips that bespeak the African heritage of their designer. What they want is to create competent engineers in the universal idiom of engineering. Of course they take their hats off to "cultural diversity," but what they mean is doing the Tarantella on Columbus Day and smashing a piñata on Cinco de Mayo. They certainly expect the new recruits to their ranks to be punctual, orderly, literate, not to interrupt their day for lunch with their family (much less for a siesta), not to allow their religious practices to interfere with their work, to hire the best qualified person for a job (not their cousin), to buy from the cheaper and more reliable supplier (not from their fellow-villager or member of the same clan). The gain of this approach is racial toleration, in which common humanity is strengthened by the imperatives of social mobility. The price is the subordination of traditional bonds and ascriptive patterns of solidarity and meaningful particularity to the injunctions of means-ends rationality. Socialization to the mores of Western industrialism is both a liberation and an uprooting. If we do not strike a balance, and that is only partly a matter of deliberate action, we risk seeing diversity reduced to some odd pieces of folklore and the addition of a few more dishes to the national cuisine.

11

Diversity and Its Discontents

Diversity is a word much in vogue, partly because it can mean different things to different people. In its ambiguity, it creates verbal agreement where, on closer inspection, there would be substantive disagreement. Its vagueness covers attitudes and policies that go further than or fall short of what the interlocutor had in mind. Verbal agreement may help advance an agenda that is not fully shared by all who are moved to support it, and obfuscation may enable decision-makers, not least academic decision-makers, to go the way of least resistance. But lack of clarity leads, above all, to self-deception.

Diversity means many things, and they are not all mutually compatible. The variety we find in great cosmopolitan centers, the Armenian tailor, the Indian restaurant, the Polish bookstore, the Chinese movie theater, not to speak of the infinity of professions, gifts, pursuits, and persuasions to be found regardless of ethnic distinctions in any city worth the name, is one thing. Regional variety—of architecture, cooking, mores, dialect—in which different parts of the world or different parts of any one country maintain a distinct character, is another. These two modes of variety can and do coexist. But if variety is a good thing, one does not "enrich" an Amish community by adding a sushi bar nor enhance a Japanese landscape by constructing a Swiss-style chalet. Nor, on the other hand, would a world be richer in which all the Armenian tailors would be found in one homogeneous city and all the Indian restaurants in another.

There is an easy optimism which conceals or plays down the very thing it purports to cherish, namely the otherness of the other. On a superficial level, embracing diversity leads to "fajita-pita" syncretism. Poor history and worse geography enhance a taste for exotic kitsch, which is the opposite of the love for the particular and the thirst for understanding the different. More seriously, the rhetorical embracing of diversity is rarely accompanied by demands for sustained intellectual effort, such as (for instance) the learning of a foreign language. Learning a foreign language is, alas, commonly viewed at best as the acquisition of a tool, rather than as a means to penetrate another intellectual universe. It is curious that just as the question of cultural diversity in university education is receiving increasing attention, be it for reasons of social policy, educational philosophy, or utility, little thought is given to this most practical and educationally valuable means of approaching the otherness of others. The learning of a foreign language is required, it would seem, of less than 20 percent of American college students.

The popularity of the term *diversity* itself is evidence of a kind of wishful thinking, for it suggests a variety within a coherent whole rather than possibly irreconcilable differences. Yet if we take culture seriously to mean a mode of being in the world, a frame of meaningful conduct, it is more than possible that elements of one culture will prove incompatible with those of another. It is not possible, for instance, to assert at the same time a universal right of cultural particularity and the universal rights of man. We cannot, to take one of many possible examples, assert at the same time a universal right to free speech and the right of religious communities, consistent with their beliefs, to execute blasphemers. Nor is it safe to believe that such excesses are limited to Islamic Fundamentalists; witness the provisions of *The Liberties of the Massachusetts Collonie in New England, of 1641,* fortunately superceded by later constitutional instruments: "If any person shall Blaspheme the name of God, the Father, Sonne or Holie Ghost, with direct, expresse, presumptuous or high-handed blasphemie, or shall curse God in the like manner, he shall be put to death."[1] Within the bounds of any single society it raises the question of the limits of toleration. How many practices can one bring under the same law without destroying the *consensus juris?*

Otherness, with all the riches that it promises and the problems that it poses must be taken seriously. It is not, as Max Weber might have put it, a taxicab that one can get in and out of at one's convenience.

Religious toleration exemplifies the capacity of liberal societies to accommodate conflicting notions of value under one law. The consensus does not adopt any one of the different ideas of the good life expressed in religious practices and teachings. As with individual rights, the law provides a formal mediation between incommensurable social practices. The state's coercive power can be neutral with regard to religious practices because, though these practices remain important—perhaps even supremely important—to those who practice them, they have no public status. Religious observance becomes an option—which is the English word for heresy—that is to say, the opposite of orthodoxy. Different substantive ideas of the good, expressed in religious practices and teachings, offer no common measure of comparison since each contends to possess or embody the standard by which to measure human practices. Religious denominations are treated equally under the law not because they have been measured against each other and found to be really equal, but in virtue of the artificial even-handedness of the law.

The same can be said of other social practices, groups and, as the jargon has it, "life-styles" that mark peoples' identities and are woven into their lives. Toleration means putting up with things that one dislikes or even disapproves of, which is why at any given place and time it is in fact only imperfectly realized. Its proper limit, however, is the law as the abstract framework of rules set up to safeguard individual rights such as life, property, and liberty, including the freedom of worship.[2]

This means that a liberal society cannot be neutral with regard to its own neutrality. To tolerate intolerance would be suicidal.

Some would contend that the short list of rights just mentioned expresses a substantive idea of the good, however limited. If so, the very limitation limits the extent and consequently the fragility of the agreement necessary to uphold them. Others again would argue that such elementary rights derive from the rule of reciprocity: "Do not do unto others . . . ," which is universalizable because it is formal. In either case the terms in which the consensus is expressed are formally abstract.

To say that the consensus of law is formal is not to say that it is an empty husk. That the "property" of the classical liberal triad (that is what is *proper* to a human being) could be replaced by "the pursuit of happiness" is evidence not only of the rhetorical genius of the writer of the Declaration of Independence, but also of the formal quality of rights that permit as they limit a variety of human responses. The formal structuring of consensus is, like language, a salutary bridge between human fallibility and human creativity.

Reciprocity or individual rights suggests that the only proper subjects of rights are individuals. The law recognizes social practices as the practices of individuals with a right to such practices and to a great variety of overlapping activities and modes of belonging, provided such activities do not unduly interfere with the rights of others under the same law.

The law, understood in this way, will not suffice by itself, as Hirsch suspected, to integrate a society. But it does indicate the limits of toleration and, conversely, the permissible limits of enforced unity.

Toleration is not relativism. In recognizing that the determination of value is not unconditional, it does not make values the objects of capricious whim. One opinion is not simply as good as another, nor is it adequately validated simply by being held. The populist, deeply anti-intellectual denial of the validity of any hierarchy of value, allowing only for psychologically motivated preferences, reflects a moral laziness which seeks to pass itself off as "freedom of conscience." The ostensibly easygoing "I'm OK, you're OK" acceptance of otherness is really a form of self-indulgent indifference toward that otherness which is neither tolerated nor embraced, but shrugged off. Otherness can be shrugged off because it is, in fact, removed from one's practical concerns, because it is so far away in some other country, or because one knows it to play within the formal rules of a liberal order, the very liberal order that the relativist considers a mere matter of opinion.[3]

"A Cretan said that all Cretans are liars." A consistent relativism is strictly impossible because it denies the basis of its own validity. It is enough to register how relativist stances are taken in the evaluation of world affairs to see how selectively they are adopted. The president wages war in Panama and Kuwait in the name of universal principles but with regard to the China of Tienanmen Square or Soviet Latvia he adopts the prudence of realpolitik: "We have our values, they have theirs." Others, repelled by the horrors of apartheid, are understandably unwilling to put it down to a different but equally valid system of South African values, but they are quite willing to ignore and sometimes even exalt analogous atrocities and exclusions in other parts of the world on the grounds of cultural relativity. What is at issue here is not the worth or prudential merit of any particular position or policy, but the impossibility of upholding both thorough-going relativism and universal values without contradiction.

A liberal order does not impose substantive pursuits. Unlike custom it does not value human beings according to their customary place or function but as free agents, within its formal framework which is itself, unlike custom, subject to deliberation.

The liberal order provides the conditions of possibility for the enactment of unique human undertakings. A human being is never just a means whose importance can be measured in terms of a contribution to some alleged common goal.

On the other hand, no society, however liberal, is constructed around the abstract norms of law alone. Human personalities are not created out of nothing. Biology aside, there is always custom and historical sedimentation. But human personalities and human destinies are nonetheless unique. No human being is merely a function of economic circumstances, of race or gender. No one is just a product of his civilization. A cultured human being, the object of a liberal education, is not just someone marked by a culture, but one who has learnt to find his way about in it and, in so doing, become aware of the conditionality of his own understanding and, indeed, of the conditionality of the particular culture itself. The integration of the inherited past with new departures, of particularity and community, of stability and change can only be achieved in the mind and psyche of each one of us. In this sense all education is student centered.

12

"O! that the Everlasting had not fix'd His canon 'gainst self-slaughter!"

The choice of the texts placed before university students has been the object of bitter contention in recent years. It is not immediately obvious why this should be so. Intellectual brawls are not new to universities. What is curious is the degree of attention paid to this brawl both inside and outside of the university. There is also nothing new about intellectuals battling over the younger generation's allegiance. What is surprising is that this allegiance can be thought to turn on a short list of a dozen books.[1] The passion with which certain readings are decried or defended can only be understood if one or both of the following obtains:

1) that the short list circumscribes the student's intellectual horizon; and

2) that the list is of symbolic rather than intellectual significance.

How limited must be the expectations of what a normal university graduate will have read or is likely to read or listen to or contemplate or otherwise consult, enjoy, or study, to think that the compulsory reading of a survey course will close the circle of her mind? What an abysmal preparation, presumably through "content-neutral" primary and secondary education, must be accepted as the norm for the battle for the students' souls to center around twelve titles? The emphasis on "animal husbandry and the mechanical arts" comes home to roost. How else can works not included in the short list be treated as "suppressed" and those included as uniquely important? Along with the intellectual abdication goes the exaltation of works to be included, on either side of this debate, not for what they say, but for what they are thought to stand for. Plato or, as the case may be, García Márquez, do not represent intellectual engagements but manifestoes, proclamations, banners.

In a characteristically vivid article, Benjamin Barber highlights the danger of an enshrined body of readings, which, like any body of writings, on an unthinking level, can serve to strengthen prejudice. "What the canon teaches is that there is a knowledge that is not conditioned by culture and interest, that is not some other century's fashion or some other culture's dominant paradigm, but which, transcending time and space, has earned the status if not of universal truth at least of universal wisdom."[2] What Barber calls the "canyon of the canon" is really a caricature. Books are written by particular people, situated in time and place. One can, of course, choose to study human utterances as expressions of a time, a place or a social condition, and, conversely, a more accurate understanding of a work can be gained by a knowledge of such circumstances. But books are not mere functions of their writers' circumstances and still less are they functions of something—collective or otherwise—purportedly more real than the writer and his work, a something of which the writer is taken to be but the mouthpiece. Understanding a work is something else than figuring out the price of grain at the time of its composition, or the class, race or gender of its author—though these may well be things we wish to examine. Identifying conditions and circumstances is, after all, itself a work of understanding. The terms in which we understand—and frequently also misunderstand—the historical world of change are not given, but are themselves conditional designations produced by our understanding. One cannot know in what terms to think, to cut up the world, before one thinks. There is no understanding prior to understanding. Texts drawn from a tradition represent, it is true, a continuity of ideas, of motifs, of images, of modes of inquiry and of symbolic forms. But it is a continuity of historical contingency, not a planned or desired unity and very far from a consistent set of beliefs. What constitutes a tradition is not substantive agreement but a formal coherence, something like a language, that makes it intelligible to those who partake of it. The same temple houses Dionysus and Apollo and for every Kant there is a Hume or a Marquis de Sade.

Unless one believes that writings and other works of the human mind are *nothing but* the reflection of interests and conditions, there is no reason why one cannot appreciate a finer composition, a more penetrating analysis, a more solidly constructed argument—and choose the readings for a university course accordingly. One can certainly do so, while recognizing the contingent conditions surrounding the emergence and, at a further remove, the influence of a work. The error consists in transforming an intellectual tradition with all the change, variety, and ambiguity it contains into a "canon" of writings to be upheld, rejected, modified, or replaced. As in the exemplary case of a canonical collection of writings, the Bible, a canon rejects some books of a tradition as spurious and accepts other books as constituting the proper foundation of a doctrine. The process is circular: the authentic books yield the true doctrine, and the books that yield the true doctrine are considered authentic. Unlike tradition, the notion of a canon implies deliberate inclusion and exclusion.

It is not quite true, on the other hand, that within a tradition, as Robert Hutchins wrote, "there is not much doubt about which are the most important voices in the Great Conversation."[3] Taking the "Great Books" series, to which Hutchins's book serves as an introduction as an example, one is inclined to wonder why, for instance, Lawrence Sterne or Henry Fielding are, but Voltaire, Pushkin, or Shelley are not among these voices.[4] Dionysius Areopagita went through more than one hundred editions in the seventeenth century. Xenophon's *Education of Cyrus*, now, alas, read only by particularly assiduous classical scholars, was endlessly read, paraphrased, imitated, and illustrated in the eighteenth century. Whereas Aeschylus made a grand return with the Romantics, the most influential single author since the Renaissance, Cicero, has declined to the point of not a single one of his works being among the Britannica's "Great Books." One could go on. The point is not to find fault with the difficult decisions that go with compiling any short list, but to note that a tradition, like a conversation, shifts its focus but maintains a continuity of reference, which alone makes the shifting foci intelligible and meaningful.

Conversation is the right word. The "canon" is a caricature also because, as its name implies, it is taken to be prescriptive. It suggests a manner of reading that is exceedingly flat. Both advocates and opponents of a canon argue as though texts were to be read as stories with a tidy moral, as lessons to be learned, as anthologies of edifying sayings to be taken to heart, or, on the contrary, as collections of insidious errors to be rejected from the presumably superior point of view of current opinion. In either case, a body of writings is supposed to amount to a consistent set of beliefs and practices. In this sense, all older books of science, for instance, are obsolete and, at the level of results, to be rejected. But if we are interested in how ideas take form in the investigator's mind, and how, in a broader perspective, we came to think the way we do, and how the way we think is part of an intellectual adventure, then they are fascinating. The matter may seem less clear in other fields, but the truth is that in ethics, aesthetics, politics, the theory of knowledge, "theories and values are not things lying about in books which one takes from them and transfers to one's own mind and soul like lifting an apple from a table to one's mouth. All reading, all education, is a dialogue, what one puts in is as important as what the other side contributes."[5] We do not read great texts in order to find conveniently formulated precepts about how to live and what to live for. Rather we make something out of ourselves, we learn to become articulate, aware of the intricacies of the human predicament as of our own predicament, by listening to the voices of the past in a mode of conversational understanding, not of prescriptive acceptance or rejection.

The world of meaningful engagements in which a university course is inscribed, the university itself, the institutions of representative government, the unfolding of discursive reason, the intricacies of technological society, the body of poetry and philosophy that makes us speak the way we do (whether we are aware of it or not) are all part of the Western tradition. We cannot choose to reject that tradition. One cannot choose one's culture, for whoever does the choosing would be no one but for his culture. The only choice is between a knowledgeable and reflective acceptance of a valuable inheritance and the thoughtless bearing of a burden. The university is itself part of the intellectual tradition of which the student partakes. The university cannot be the neutral conveyor of "cultures." It can and indeed must convey knowledge of other cultures but it cannot but convey them in the intellectual idiom characteristic of a university—that is, of a historically and culturally specific, though not unchanging, institution. The idea of somehow non- or pre-culturally prefabricated selves shopping around for mix-and-match cultures is surely an illusion, which, among other things, gets in the way of developing a true respect for other cultures. The university has, sadly, frequently served as a focus for consciousness raising in the service, for instance, of nationalism in its many forms. The transition from elite to mass higher education inevitably transferred an even greater burden on the universities as agents of socialization which was until now the (not unproblematic) domain of primary and secondary schools. That means that the always fragile independence of academic work is under greater pressure to satisfy ideological demands for "political correctness" and for "other-centered studies," not as the cultivation of previously neglected fields, but as the methodological presupposition of inquiry.

The question arises whether, at a time when an increasing proportion of the American population is not of Western origin, the parameters of a liberal education need not be widened to take into account non-Western traditions. Bearers of such traditions, their integration into American society notwithstanding, have drawn great strength from them. I. M. Pei was interviewed by Diane Sawyer on *60 Minutes* at the time when he was building the glass pyramid of the Louvre. She asked him how he felt about the French being affronted or condescending toward an American architect, from what to their eyes was a young and uncouth country, tampering with one of the temples of French culture. "Ah," he answered, "but I am *Chinese*-American!" But Pei was born a high-class mandarin and did not pick up Chinese civilization and the pride that goes with it at an American school. On a more modest level, the tension between the pull of integration and the awareness of belonging to a distinctive tradition is more problematic. The demand for broadening the cultural parameters of education has to do with the perceived need for recognition of the equal dignity of cultures as markers of identity, a task frequently made difficult by the coincidence of class and ethnicity. The matter is complicated further because culture is often used as a euphemism for race. But culture is not genetic, it is historical and social.

It is always a good thing to expand one's horizon of information and, more importantly, the range of one's understanding. If people of different origins bring with them the elements and, at the same time, stimulate by their very presence an interest in the cultural wealth that they represent, the experience can only be enriching. To be aroused from a complacent self-congratulation and unexamined confidence in the intrinsic superiority of one's own way of doing things and be made aware of the conditionality of one's own system of values by being reminded of the richly varied particularity of human modes of existence, is entirely salutary. Conversely, it is very supportive for the minority student (soon, in California, for instance, to be a plurality student) looking at a curriculum to find a prima facie answer to the question: "Where am *I* in all this?" But since the demands are primarily psychological, aiming less at cognition than at recognition, the responses are largely symbolic. The danger is then grandstanding tokenism and superficiality. The proper understanding of another culture requires a long apprenticeship. If one turns one's attention to it, the less familiar can, with patience, be assimilated in terms of what is already familiar. Quick souvenir-hunting expeditions may be politically opportune, but they are educationally worthless. Learning *about* a culture is, furthermore, something other than adopting its ways. We only understand in terms of what is already understood. Acculturation need not be a one-way street, and the majority culture can adapt to accommodate what is at first alien as well as the other way round. But the "mainstream" tradition cannot for all that be cancelled, and even if that were possible, there are very good reasons why it would not be desirable. We return to the limits of toleration of a liberal order.

The university can make available cultural goods from the four corners of the world, instill respect for otherness and remind us that homogeneity offers not only mobility and opportunity but also boring and stultifying sameness. But it cannot and should not deny its own origin as an institution rooted in the Western tradition and dedicated to the disinterested pursuit of truth.

13

Innocents Abroad

A large, powerful, rich, and in many ways self-sufficient country like the U.S., is easily tempted to close upon itself.

History and geography have been good to the U.S. Placed between two oceans and two weak neighbors, it could afford historically to think of war, except for civil war, as something that took place elsewhere. Technology changed that. Pearl Harbor was a portent. As it turned out, technological superiority, demonstrated most dramatically by the Bomb, succeeded in keeping the war at a distance from the national territory and the civilian population, and resolved the conflict in America's favor. Military superiority could then be viewed not only as an instrument of national security, but also as a means of maintaining the old possibility of isolation. No one in his right mind would quarrel with the need to provide for the common defense. What is problematic is the nostalgic desire for a shield—a shield in the sky perhaps—to prevent the complications of a messy world from being thrust upon American life.

In the economic sphere as well, America's natural resources and its vast internal market made it possible for Americans to think of international exchanges with an equanimity quite unthinkable for countries, both rich and poor, vitally dependent on foreign trade. It is not that the United States has not been active, indeed extremely active, in international economic matters. It is rather that the man in the street considered foreign involvement an optional extra until the repercussions of an increasingly integrated world economy began to be plainly visible at home. American engagement in world trade is, of course, very old, congenital one might say with the planting of colonies on these shores. From the notorious triangular trade, to the China clippers of New England, to the building of the railroads with a great deal of foreign capital and imported labor, to oil exploration and extraction, to the establishment of major manufacturing subsidiaries abroad, to international finance, America has never been absent from the world market. But this involvement was overshadowed by the magnitude of western expansion and domestic industrialization. Perceptions began to change only when it became apparent that America was not just an actor on the world scene but an integral part of a world market, which it has largely helped to bring about. It is now clear for all to see that it is itself open to other actors, and that not only in terms of marginal cheap or luxury imports, but in central areas of manufacturing, banking, and real estate. The response has sometimes been unseemly and short-sighted xenophobia. That is a shame on a number of counts, because international engagement is not an option that one can take up when the terms seem favorable and turn down when they don't. It is an inexorable fact of modern life.

The prudence or morality of particular overseas enterprises, of their proper nature and extent is, naturally, always open to debate. There is no denying, however, that the United States is inevitably and permanently enmeshed in a complex world in which its inaction as a Great Power can be as significant as its action. Though the scope and manner of its engagement in the world may change, it cannot choose to withdraw. Foreign misadventures or what is frequently perceived as an excessive preoccupation with foreign affairs leads to calls for America to "come home." The public as a whole seems to regard foreign affairs as either satisfactory or embarrassing but always as somehow extraordinary operations of little interest, unless they assume the rousing quality of a "crusade" (with correspondingly intense responses when they go wrong).

American government reflects this attitude. George Kennan has pointed out "the unsuitability of the American governmental system for the promulgation of any sustained administrative program (particularly one calling for annual appropriations of sizeable sums of money) that was not supported at all times by the enthusiasm of some internal domestic pressure group" and attributes it to the "lack of comprehension for the nature and exigencies of the diplomatic function on the part of a great continental society not accustomed to regard prospering foreign relations as important."[1] Considerable sums are spent, of course, on foreign affairs (leaving aside military expenditure), but ad hoc, on foreign aid, special missions, summits, not on regular professional diplomacy. The State Department itself was formed in preference to one for foreign affairs because it was thought that the job of the latter would become obsolete after the establishment of "perpetual" treaties of commerce with other nations. In the early years of the Republic one representative put it like this: "a time would come when the United States would be disengaged from the necessity of supporting a Secretary of Foreign Affairs"![2] Foreigners never cease to wonder at the indifference, sometimes experienced as an affront, manifest in appointing personalities, distinguished or otherwise, with no background in foreign affairs, much less an attachment to the Foreign Service, to head diplomatic missions with the sole purpose of paying off domestic political debts. It is frequently said in defense of this practice that in this day of telecommunications, ambassadors have lost much of their importance. True as this is, the reliance on impersonal information and expertise, the idea that one can do without a capable man or woman on the spot who can really get to know a place and report home, is itself evidence of a simplified view, which regards the world, at least insofar as it concerns America, as fundamentally homogeneous. The ancient instinct of America is to recoil from a messy world, in habits formed by its once "detached and distant situation" as Washington put it in his Farewell Address, jealously guarding against "the insidious wiles of foreign influence." But then Washington still believed that it was possible to extend commercial relations while having "as little political connection as possible."

In 1920 Warren Harding, while looking with satisfaction at "the new order of the world" chose to interpret his success at the polls as a "referendum . . . rejecting internationality" and as a mandate for "the resumption of our inward normal way."[3] And never does averting one's gaze from the rest of the world, with its challenges and opportunities, its problems and its horrors appear so normal as during an election year, for there are no electoral votes to be gained overseas.

To go out on the town when one chooses to, but to stay at home when one wants to be left alone, is an understandable desire. If it was ever politically or economically possible for the United States (or any other country for that matter), it is now quite out of the question. For one thing, it has become increasingly difficult to tell exactly what is inside and what is outside. Multinational corporations have become more so, not only in the location of their manufacturing and marketing operations but even in management and control. When a borrower defaults on a loan in Argentina, it endangers a depositor in Schenectady; a poor crop in the Ukraine means high prices for an Iowa farmer; and what happens to the Amazonian forest can change the weather in Peoria. Nothing could be more truly global than the danger of nuclear destruction. None of this is exactly new (even the Bomb is almost half a century old), but the links were never so clear, the responsibilities so pressing and, by the same token, perhaps, the opportunities so great.

The nature and the extent of international engagement will differ, of course, according to circumstances. To the extent that such engagement can be the subject of deliberate action, it should be the object of informed deliberation. What will not do is to pretend that the rest of the world can be turned off, or that it is "really" just like America and therefore requires no special understanding. More dangerous still is the notion that the world can be re-formed in America's image so that one can deal with those benighted foreigners as one would with the folks down home. The logic of economic rationality is easily mistaken for the American way. Anyone who has tried to do business in Japan or even Europe can attest to the fact that the overlap is only partial.

In the years after World War II, when the rest of the industrial world was in ashes, it was possible for American industry to deal with the rest of the world more or less on its own terms. Its colossal success was due in great part, of course, to intrinsic technical and organizational virtues, but it was undoubtedly aided by the overwhelming political preponderance of the U.S., and the benefits of a large domestic market. Time has eroded, without eliminating, these advantages, but attitudes formed in those days still linger. A further source of complacency is the currency of English as the lingua franca of commerce and increasingly also of scientific exchange throughout the world. The historical accident of one English-speaking hegemonic power succeeding another, convenient as it is, can also mislead English speakers into thinking that the world is more homogeneous than it is, as they perceive it through the unifying lens of their native tongue. The non-native speakers, having broken through the eggshell of their own language, have in that respect the upper hand: they know more about the native English-speakers than the latter do about the former.

In order to deal competently and responsibly with the rest of the world, one must know about it. First, then, one must, above all, be willing to learn about it. The level of information of American students about the rest of the world is appalling. Ignorance breeds indifference. The lack of terms of reference kills curiosity. It is a vicious circle. True, many young people travel, and that is all to the good. Others join the Peace Corps and have a more real and often sobering experience of other places. But on the whole students, and especially engineering students, tend to stay at home, locked into tight study schedules, local internships, and interviews with prospective employers. Countless opportunities for foreign study, scholarships, and exchanges go begging. Advisors rarely mention such opportunities.[4] Only when the employers make it clear that applicants with foreign experience have an advantage will the schools and the students respond. Needless to say, here as in other fields, American students are poorly served by their elementary and secondary preparation. Solid and sufficiently broad geographical knowledge is sorely lacking. Even the acquisition of a measure of familiarity with a single other region or country and its civilization would be invaluable. When, given at least one other point of reference, the self-reflective closure of one's own civilization is overcome, the path to understanding many more is open. To help achieve this is also part of a liberal education.

14

Manifest Destiny vs.
the Serpent Columbus

Americans, who have good reason to cherish their institutions, were well advised, no doubt, to guard against "the insidious wiles of foreign influence," which, as Washington warned in his Farewell Address, history and experience have proven to be "one of the most baneful foes of republican government." A "chosen country," said Thomas Jefferson in his first Inaugural, "with room enough for our descendants to the thousandth and thousandth generation," America was fortunate to have been "kindly separated by nature and a wide ocean from the exterminating havoc" of Europe and to avoid "entanglements"—except for those it could engage in with impunity in Latin America, for example, or the Philippines—for as long as it was able to do so.

The separate and "chosen" situation of America is not, however, a mere empirical fact but becomes part of a myth that views the United States as the culmination or the privileged vehicle of a providential development of world-historical significance. Like all true myths it has several versions, some more overtly religious, some more secular. Leaving behind the turmoil and oppression of the Old World, man is reborn in the New World, and the New Adam finds equality, freedom, and prosperity in the New World. Turning its collective back on the European Babylon, the Chosen People erects a new Zion, a new Jerusalem from "sea to shining sea." Western expansion is an integral part of this movement: the western course of empire or Pilgrim feet, who "with impassioned stress, the thoroughfare of Freedom beat across the wilderness."

Everything that modern man dreamt of seems to come together in the triumphant sweep of one progressive movement: equality of conditions in a land of plenty, freedom of conscience, political liberty, superstition retreating before rationality, mastery over nature and self-determination, unlimited opportunity inviting the spirit of enterprise to ever greater feats. In short, the American Dream appears as Manifest

Destiny. The myth is lived in the isolationist mode, seeking to keep the providential promise uncontaminated, held up as an example for those with eyes to see, or, more actively, in the missionary mode, seeking to spread the message, making the world safe for democracy. Either way, the experience is taken to be exemplary. The events leading up to it are significant as steps toward the accomplishment of an appointed end, as stations or contributions to the realization of the promise of mankind. The sailing of Columbus is seen as the most important and epoch-making voyage in human history. It is a "triumph of the human spirit," and was properly celebrated in the Columbian exhibition of 1892.[1]

As we reach the five hundredth anniversary of that momentous landfall, a different view is being put about. Rather than lead out of the vale of tears, the modern project is leading straight to hell. Technological progress, the rule of law, political stability, consumer affluence, individual autonomy, citizenship, rational management, "really" means environmental damage, social conformism, covert oppression, concentration of wealth, crass inequalities, political powerlessness before bureaucratic authority, and the danger of mass destruction.

Western man has eaten of the tree of knowledge and lost his innocence. Descartes, whose science aimed to make man "master and possessor of nature," has, in fact, laid out the organization of the sciences in the well-known image of a tree.[2]

Columbus appears as the embodiment of budding modern European technology and capitalism: guns and sails,[3] capital accumulation needed to outfit expeditions that would, with the prospect of further profit, penetrate virgin lands in order to exploit them. The discovery and colonization of America is not a mere episode of European expansion but a decisive stimulus, both a means by which and a field in which it is realized. The leading country established on its shores by Europeans finally becomes itself the foremost, that is in this view the farthest gone, agent of exploitative, technocratic, imperialist capitalism. The redemptive myth of America has its damning countermyth. The "Admiral of the Ocean Sea" opened to rape and genocide and exploitation a continent of hitherto peace-loving natives living in close-knit communities, in harmony with nature and with each other. He laid it bare to the selfishly individualist, ruthlessly accumulative, calculating spirit of Europe, out to use people and nature alike as mere objects of its insatiable appetite. The serpent had entered the Garden of Eden.[4]

Clearly, neither myth nor counter-myth is history. Columbus was not the harbinger of paradise on earth. Crossing the Atlantic is not like crossing the font. Settlers in America, though often fleeing evils in

Europe, did not leave evil behind them. What they found were opportunities and hardships and more or less accommodating institutions—indeed, in general comparison, institutions sometimes incomparably more rather than less accommodating. They found (or founded) admirable though, naturally, imperfect institutions and otherwise struggled with the mixture of good and evil that human beings always carry within them.

Neither did evil need to be imported to the New World. The European discovery of America was, unquestionably, a disaster for the discovered. To draw attention to the lives and the meaningfully human ways of life of those who were destroyed is certainly a worthy task and an important counterweight to widespread indifference or callousness that tends to write them off as "collateral damage" (to use the latest euphemism) of the sweep of "progress."

But only a narrowing down of evil to the evils characteristic, or thought to be characteristic, of technological civilization and a willfully sentimental understanding of living "close to nature," can imagine that Pre-Columbian America knew no evil. The admiral's own description of the Caribs that first met him as timid and childlike serves as the standard starting point of the paradisic images currently being brought forward. Columbus may, of course, have been trying to persuade his royal patrons of the ease with which the islands he had claimed in their name could be conquered and held, just as he tried to persuade them that it was worthwhile to do so by writing of gold-bearing rivers flowing through these same islands. Be that as it may, and allowing timidity to pass for goodness, there is little doubt that the organized societies of the American mainland, the Aztecs, the Incas, and (as we now know) the Mayas, were capable of the most fearful oppression and the most bloodcurdling cruelty. Cortez could conquer Mexico because so many downtrodden subjects of the Aztecs greeted him as a liberator.

Columbus, the conquistadors, the settlers of North America are easy to debunk if they are first inflated into peerless images pointing to the sunny uplands of our current bliss, icons serving the self-congratulation of white Americans. It is tempting to set up countericons. But it is better to tell the truth. Only if one assumes that the students and the people can never know the truth can one argue otherwise. Such a conviction, which puts everything in the hands of the "image-makers," is sadly self-realizing.

The truth about Columbus is that he was a superb mariner, a greedy and ambitious man of low birth, who dreamt of setting himself and his descendants up as Grandees of Spain by means of his exploits. The exploits themselves are astounding and the results, for better and for worse, momentous. They were made possible, of course, by circumstances, technical, financial, political, social, and personal. Without these circumstances Columbus would not have sailed. But it was Columbus, not capitalism, who picked up the trade winds and landed in Hispaniola.

To the extent that a liberal education is historical, that is, to a very considerable extent, it is not charged with playing one myth against another and showing events to be instances of some purportedly all-encompassing explanatory scheme, but of explaining events in context, in terms of contemporary happenings insofar as such things can be ascertained. Patterns, if patterns there be, emerge from evidence in response to a question. It is valuable to develop a sense of what counts as evidence in response to what kind of question and to suspend judgment until the evidence is in. The rest is ideology.

15

Babylonian Captivity and the Suffering Servant

Readers of Montaigne will remember that the ways of Western nations will appear as strange and absurd to cannibals as those of cannibals appear to Europeans. "There is nothing barbarous and savage," he wrote, about the natives of the newly discovered America, "except that each man calls barbarism whatever is not his own practice; for indeed it seems we have no other test of truth and reason than the example and pattern of the opinions and customs of the country we live in."[1]

Montaigne's observation points to two characteristics of Western thought. The first is the capacity and the will to step outside the circle of one's own polity and culture and, by adopting the perspective of an outsider, to hold up a mirror to one's own society. Naturally, what is involved is a thought experiment, but it is more than a mere literary device. Herodotus, who places the discussion on the best form of government in the mouths of Persian nobles, Aeschylus who makes Salamis a drama experienced by Persians, Montesquieu in his *Lettres Persanes,* do not become Persian, but the possibility of empathy and of adopting the others' point of view is given in principle. The explorer, the traveler, the anthropologist "go native" only intermittently and up to a degree—or their story would be lost to the rest of us. But their story points to the possibility of an independent judgment, arrived at by comparison, that is by more than conformity to one's community custom. "So we may well call these people barbarians, in respect to the rules of reason, but not in respect to ourselves, who surpass them in every kind of barbarity."[2]

What the comparison yields is less a universally valid rule than a warning against idolatry: no society of fallible human beings lives by the absolute truth.

This leads us to the second characteristic manifest in Montaigne: the awareness, resulting from comparison, of the conditionality of our understanding, that is of its dependence on cultural terms of reference.

We are aware that our values, our beliefs about good and evil, our identity do not emerge in a vacuum. We are conscious of the social nature of human beings. Our human experience is necessarily an experience we share with other human beings and it is therefore formed by the language, the way of thinking, the emotional climate and the material conditions of our surroundings. We are what we are in great part because we are recognized by others as being this rather than that. Cognition cannot be divorced from recognition. The "self-made man" is an illusion.

But so is the man "creature of his circumstances." It is impossible to maintain a sense of human dignity if one believes that a personality is no more than a coordinate of impersonal forces. Puppets are not responsible: they deserve neither praise nor blame. A human being who is nothing but an expression of social relationships is, strictly speaking, worthless: she is nothing, and the social relationships are everything. In a deterministic scheme of things, a liberal education, diversity and all, is not just impossible; it is meaningless.

That is, of course, precisely what Marx maintained: freedom, culture, law are only superficial forms, screening the underlying reality of class conflict. If Marx is right, we delude ourselves when we think we are providing a liberal education. The culture that we wish to transmit and the passing of which we lament is only class culture, "the outgrowth of the conditions of . . . bourgeois production and bourgeois property" and "for the enormous majority, a mere training to act as a machine."[3] We have seen that many of the side effects of a liberal education are in fact very useful, indeed essential to the efficient functioning of a technological society. If that were all it accomplished, a liberal education would be indeed a misnomer. If, furthermore, the operation of the machine is considered, as it is by Marxists, not morally neutral, capable, that is, of producing good or bad results depending on how it is guided, but intrinsically oppressive, then such an education is downright evil. One's duty to humanity would then be to advance not a liberal but a liberating education, that is to foment revolution.

This puts us in something of a double bind, for if our consciousness is class consciousness determined by the relations of production, how can we hope to raise ourselves, in Marx's words "to the level of comprehending theoretically the historical movement as a whole"?[4] If we are capable of theoretical understanding, that is of detachment, then we are no longer determined, but free.

Marxists have generally sought to escape this contradiction in two ways: by adopting a watered-down version of determinism and by postulating the possibility (and need) of a revolutionary avant-garde. According to the first, instead of Marx's famous straightforward statement from the preface of the *Critique of Political Economy* to the effect that "it is not the consciousness of men that determines their existence, but on the contrary their social existence determines their consciousness," you postulate that the external conditions of your life affect the way you think and conversely the way you think acts back on the way you live. This is, of course, difficult to deny, but what the proposition gains in plausibility it loses in explicative power. It becomes impossible to know what explains from what is being explained. The art of presenting this kind of inconclusive circularity as capable of yielding valid conclusions is called "dialectics."

The idea of the avant-garde means that certain chosen people, in practice always a self-appointed elite, are, despite the operation of deterministic laws, ahead of their time and can look back, as it were, on the present and lead the masses who, the vanguard knows, cannot hope to understand their situation, given the "objective circumstances" that dim their vision, into the future. In some versions it is the revolution itself that transforms the consciousness of the revolutionaries, that provides the "objective conditions" of a revolutionary consciousness achieved in the crucible of violence. Alienation, the separation of theory and praxis, is overcome in the absolute praxis of violence. Education as a means to unify a personality, to make it whole is then an exercise in consciousness raising. Formal education will be ineffective. Action, the revolution itself, will be the reliable teacher. Whatever can be said in favor of this view it cannot, by its very terms, be defended in reason. But then this activism, where Right meets Left in its opposition to the liberal order, considers reason a bourgeois prejudice.

The hopes connected with revolution go beyond the hope of righting particular wrongs of which there are, alas, only too many. Revolutionary hope rests rather on the conviction that man is not *essentially* a broken vessel and that he *can* be made whole by human action. Marx is probably right to believe that different modes of production are linked to different modes of alienation, but he believes that alienation itself is not part of the human condition but the effect of contingent, though in his scheme of things historically necessary, social relations.

> The selfish misconception that induces you [i.e., the bourgeois] to transform into eternal laws of nature and of reason, the social forms springing from your present form of property—historical relations that rise and disappear in the progress of production—this misconception you share with every ruling class that has preceded you.[5]

There is a messianic expectation linked with the "last" suffering class in Marxian history, the industrial proletariat. Marked by its very suffering, it is historically destined to effect the last upheaval in history thus abolishing history as the history of class struggle. The rule of man over man will disappear, and man will no longer be separated from the product of his work nor splintered by the division of labor. Man, or at least "species-man," will overcome alienation and be whole again. In redeeming itself, the suffering class will redeem mankind.

For all metastatic prophecies since Isaiah, a suffering servant of the Master of Providence is the chosen vehicle of the transformation of the human condition. The emancipation and homecoming of the chosen people liberates and unifies mankind.[6]

In this regard, more than in any other, the Marxian prophecy has failed. The proletariat did not prove to be the vehicle chosen by History to liberate itself and thereby "all flesh" from the Babylonian captivity of capitalism and to effect man's repatriation from the exile of aliena-tion. "Capitalism" did not bring about its own destruction. Contrary to Marx's prediction, the modern laborer *did* rise with the progress of modern industry rather than "[sink] deeper and deeper below the con-ditions of existence of his own class."[7] Pauperism did not develop more rapidly than population and wealth. The development of modern in-dustry did not "cut from under its feet the very foundation on which the bourgeoisie produces and appropriates products" nor did "the bourgeoisie produce its own grave-diggers." The "victory of the prole-tariat," far from being "inevitable" became immaterial, as the indus-trial proletariat was absorbed into the middle classes, and to the joy of some, including the new bourgeois themselves, and to the distress of others, acquired "bourgeois" tastes and habits.

What did remain behind, at least in America, was what has come to be called an "underclass" (that is not properly or in the Marxian sense a class at all—how else to account, in Marx's terms, for a class below the *last* class?), which Marx had described with characteristic disdain: "the 'dangerous class,' the social scum [*Lumpenproletariat*], that passively rotting mass thrown off by the lowest ranges of old society,"[8] which Marx considered a more likely ally of reaction than of revolution.

On the other hand, the spread of the industrial mode of produc-tion—albeit sometimes under the label of "socialism"—over the whole surface of the globe, the creation of a world market, the concomitant retreat of emotive, traditional, hierarchical social relations before im-personal exchanges marked by the "cash nexus" announced in *The Communist Manifesto,* are all undeniably part of today's world. Allowing for the pejorative use of the term *bourgeois,* there is little doubt that all nations have been compelled "on pain of extinction, to adopt the bourgeois mode of production" and compelled to introduce what it calls civilization into their midst, i.e., to become bourgeois themselves." The industrial mode of production therefore "creates a world after its own image."9

Whether this development is lamentable or whether it gives reasons for satisfaction will depend on whether one believes the mode of production to be the sole determinant of the "social being" of individuals and nations, leveling everything properly cultural before it, or whether significant particularities and voluntary and affective bonds between people can find their place in the new scheme of things—in some respects perhaps an even more important place because of the emancipation from the automatism of custom. It will depend on whether one expects that the new prosperity will eventually embrace rather than pauperize the disadvantaged, those whom industrialism has marginalized by assuming center stage and whom it can no longer leave alone, for better or for worse. It depends, that is, on whether the further development of industrial society with regard to the disadvantaged will follow the pattern predicted by Marx for the proletariat, or the pattern of inclusion or cooptation that actually emerged.

Industrial society has "created enormous cities" and "greatly increased the urban population as compared with the rural" beyond the wildest imagination of the nineteenth century. There is no question that a great deal of what is vibrant, varied, and urbane about modern society is linked to urban life, but in the face of the squalor and misery that is the other side of city life, we can hardly be as confident as Marx that urbanization "has thus rescued a considerable part of the population from the idiocy of rural life."10 Some would maintain, furthermore, that the sprawl of suburbs is creating a new idiocy of its own.

Treated with sufficient elasticity, or perhaps dialectical acumen, the Marxian analysis could be rescued, it seems, if only a universally revolutionary suffering class could be found to take the place of the disappearing industrial proletariat as the bearer of humanity's messianic hopes. The "New Left," which flourished in the sixties, found such a class in what Frantz Fanon, borrowing the title of his book from the first line of the *Internationale,* called *Les damnés de la terre.*11 By that he meant the impoverished populations of the Third World and the blacks of American inner cities.

The sufferings and deprivations are real enough. But they were given a new meaning in the context of a new or renewed metastatic myth.

16

Separation as Collective Therapy

The Marxian analysis was adapted in a number of ways. Class as the focus of historical struggle and development was complemented by race, colonial rule, and, eventually, gender. The determining "social being" of man was taken to have a broader base than economic relations and to include, or even to consist primarily of cultural forms of domination or, as Gramsci put it, "hegemony." Finally, psychoanalytic theories were brought to bear on the anthropological side of alienation.

Black activists, impatient, suspicious, finally cynical toward the gradualism of the American polity, developed a psychologically centered idea of black pride, which asserted the distinctive difference of blacks. Unlike Martin Luther King, who in his famous speech from the Lincoln Memorial in August of 1963 dreamt of a day when "the sons of former slaves and the sons of former slave-holders will be able to sit down together at the table of brotherhood," the younger radicals rejected integration. Assimilation, their experience told them, meant adopting a white ethos, the stereotypical expressions of which were precisely responsible for damaging the self-esteem of blacks. A defiant assertion of separateness and racial pride manifest in the "Black Power" campaign of the sixties and seventies appeared, then, as the means for overcoming a self-abnegation imposed by hostile social surroundings.

The removal of formal legal and political barriers, as a result of the Civil Rights movement, had revealed other social barriers. It revealed above all the persistence of racism, which, with the abolition of its official enforcement, could no longer be mistaken for a monopoly of a racist South but was seen to be equally present in the school busing crisis of Boston or the Watts riots in Los Angeles. The visible disparity of socioeconomic opportunities, the de facto segregation of black ghetto versus white suburb, made a mockery of the egalitarian pretensions of a white America, unable—at least at the time—to satisfy expectations aroused by its own image of itself.

Black leaders who, unlike King, had no time for slow, painful progress, much less for the redemptive power of suffering, responded by transforming the social drama of their experience into a Manichaean psychodrama. Racism, they read in Fanon, is not an individual attitude, a contingent aspect of human conduct. It is rather an integral element of white culture, merely the most visible part of the "white power structure." It is an instrument and an expression of white domination over people of color. White America is in this respect the equivalent of European colonial powers. There is, then, no point in seeking piecemeal ameliorations nor in holding particular individuals responsible. It is taken to be an inescapable structural fact.

That is, one suspects, one of the chief reasons why this view has gained a considerable amount of credence among whites as well. When structural determinations are at work, no one in particular is responsible. One can afford to occupy the psychologically gratifying high ground of a guilt that, being collective, leaves one off the hook as an individual. Conversely, structural determinism makes it possible to claim that all whites, qua participants and automatic beneficiaries of the structure of power, are inevitably racist, whereas blacks, as the victims of oppression, are never racist, regardless of the hatred and contempt they may harbor and express in word and deed against members of other races qua members of other races. It is evident that such a view is incompatible with any notion of individual responsibility, which presupposes, of course, that there is always a modicum of free will in human beings. To maintain the opposite, if one only looks at the shape of the cage of determination from a different angle, amounts to saying that there can be no such thing as a criminal, because, in a sense, it is always "society's fault."

The disproportionate number of blacks in jail suggests that it is not just their individual perversity that put them there, but it would be hardly fair to people facing similar difficulties and leading regular upright lives to think that they are simply "dupes of the system" or that crooks are nothing but victims of oppression.

Frantz Fanon's expression of the black experience, and, by extension, of the experience of any group regarding itself as "colonized," has become canonical or, if one prefers, anticanonical. He is the only author to appear twice on the most politically correct of the revised short lists of Stanford's new Civilizations, Ideas, Values (CIV) course.[1] The emphasis is on the psychological dimensions of the dynamics of colonization. The experience of a black man "making it" in the European world shows that he doesn't cease to be viewed as black even as he seeks to become more and more "white." The experience of a Stokely Carmichael (as he then was)[2]—like Fanon, a West Indian by birth—of "making it" in white America, lionized by "progressive" white school-mates and their families because he was an intelligent, articulate *black,* is quite similar. Integration appears as the adoption of a mask whose features mock those of the "real" person underneath.[3]

The psychic split, which incapacitates the Negro, is seen to result from a social situation in which he is regarded as belonging to a group by virtue of an indelible, external mark of recognition, the color of his skin. The psychological distortion is only indirectly a personal trauma, being rather a function of the status of an entire group. To achieve freedom, the black man needs to be recognized as a man by other men. He will attain this not by trying to be co-opted into a world of "Euro-centric" values, but by manly struggle. A collective ill requires a collec-tive therapy. The antithesis of revolution to be undertaken by the new international proletariat of the colonized against the thesis of colonial dominance will lead to the synthesis of a new world harmony. By liberating himself, the colored man will liberate mankind, restoring the psychic peace presumed to have existed before the Europeans and their technology destroyed it. For in this "dialectical" scheme of things, the Europeans are themselves victims of history. The black man's aliena-tion derives from European Negrophobia.[4] If, as Fanon knew from Sartre, it is anti-Semitism that makes the Jew, it is the white men's fear of the blacks that make the Nigger.[5] The European fear of blacks derives, according to Fanon the psychiatrist and reader of Richard Wright, from sexual repression. The technological and organizational achievements that enabled Europeans to dominate the world was bought at the price of sublimation. This, Fanon tells us, is not a universal mechanism of human culture, but a specifically European hang-up. Blacks, he maintains, at any rate West Indian blacks, have no Oedipus complex and are quite free of sexual deviation.[6] To the European subconscious, blackness stands for all that is elemental, sinful, and dangerous. Black alienation results from absorption of European alien-ated consciousness, along with European language, culture, and tech-nology. The liberation of the suffering servant will liberate mankind. The head of the serpent will be crushed, and essence and existence will come together.

17

The Crustacean Theory of Culture

Violence is the natural expression of an existentialist attempt to achieve psychic integrity by means of engaged action. Linked to the racial stereotype of Negro potency it became for an Eldridge Cleaver, self-proclaimed "loudmouthed nigger, ex-convict, rapist, advocate of violence, Presidential candidate," the ramrod of racial emancipation.[1] Yet violence is only the extreme manifestation of a deliberate closure in which liberation is viewed as a psychological catharsis in the form of a full identification with people like oneself. "Likeness" is defined by the one decisive mark, taken to be the differentia of the group, to the exclusion of others. The tactical aim may not be as grand as the one postulated by Fanon, and may instead aim at positioning a group in the distributive system of a settled society. Yet, Stokely Carmichael's slogan, "Before a group can enter the open society, it must first close ranks," still seems to serve the psychological satisfaction of defiant solidarity better than the political success of African Americans. Closure prevents not only the integration into "mainstream" society of several individuals as such, but also the finding of political allies for the group as a whole. It is perhaps no accident that the Reverend Jesse Jackson was calling for a "rainbow coalition."

The calls to violence have abated since the sixties, and the vast majority of African Americans stayed closer to the traditional reformist voices of the Civil Rights movement than to the more radical version of black nationalism. But the vocabulary of group identity, of human identity determined by belonging to groups marked by external signs has entered the language and taken cover under the broad wing of "diversity."

Human beings are thought to be who they are in terms of exoskeletal categories such as race, class, and gender and to be true to themselves insofar as they are true to this kind of crustacean identity. Such categories are posited as prior to reason itself, not as phenomena to be understood, but as the heuristic instruments by means of which we must see the world, if we are to see it correctly. The elasticity of the term *diversity* makes it possible to accommodate these, in principle exclusionary, and ultimately solipsistic, categories within the compass of a political culture which appeals to toleration, inclusion, participation and autonomy. The autonomy claimed in the name of exoskeletal groups is, however, not that of individual human beings as the proper subjects of rights and capable of different modes of belonging, but of groups as claimants to entitlements and of individuals only insofar as they are members of the pertinent groups. The public recognition of certain groups as "protected," however justified in terms of public policy or distributive justice, tends to freeze recognition and self-recognition in certain molds. In important respects, that restricts diversity more than it enhances it. The exaltation of exclusive determinative collective partic- ularities runs counter to the idea of a society consisting of diverse indi- viduals. A society the members of which, that is, the ultimate pertinent bearers of interest and will—the elementary units to be represented—are not individual human beings but collectivities will be at best a federation and more likely a battlefield. There are countries such as Lebanon where, for historical reasons, religious, linguistic, ethnic, and tribal distinctions actually constitute meaningfully integrated and mutually exclusive com- munities. Ingenious devices are required to compose their differences, such as a prearranged apportionment of government offices, veto pow- ers, and employment and patronage quotas. There are places, such as the Netherlands or Switzerland, where such devices are successful for long periods of time and other places, such as South Africa perhaps, where their adoption might be advisable.[2] Western societies, in Europe no less than in America, are facing difficult problems of ethnicity. National cultures are challenged by "counter-entropic" groups, marked by racial or cultural traits, such as color and language, and who are prevented from assimilating to the functional "high" culture or unable to do so. Given the universalist embrace of the modern industrial na- tion, they can no longer live without friction in a subordinate or mar- ginal position with regard to the functional mainstream. Unlike the French-speaking Quebecois, for example, they also lack any realistic possibility of setting up on their own or plausibly threatening to do so. They appear, therefore, on the political scene as non-negotiable collec- tive entities advancing claims of recognition and advancement of the group as such and of their members in their quality as members of such a group. It remains to be seen in what measure the familiar American pattern of rising out of one's group rather than with it will operate.

"It is a characteristic difference between a league and a government" wrote Publius, that the authority of the Union extend "to the persons of the citizens—the only proper objects of government."[3] Intermediate bodies, state and local governments, associations of different sorts, classes even can, as Tocqueville pointed out, enhance participation in the public life of a country and need not be feared as splintering the citizen body of the Republic, "one and indivisible." It is difficult, however, to see why any society, having the choice, would wish to subvert the principle of the individual citizen as the proper ultimate subject of representation and adopt a policy designed *to bring about* a kind of internal Balkanization. The reason why "cultural diversity," in the sense of adapting the polity itself to accommodate *non-negotiable* group identities, is embraced with such passion, is that it provides a vocabulary ostensibly compatible with a political culture inclined to toleration, inclusion, and participation to advance claims of advancement and power likely to devolve not so much on the individuals composing the group in question, but on those who advance claims in its name. The exoskeletal theory of culture implies a lack or radical denial of a common world of reference, and of the individual as the proper last unit—however mediated—composing society. Where the values around which each group coheres are radically incommensurable with those of other groups and the notion of even a minimal formal network of law encompassing them all is denied as itself "bourgeois," "Eurocentric," and false, there can be nothing but the game of power. If this is so, there is no sense of speaking of rights and wrongs, individual or collective, no giving to each his own. Appeals to justice are then only tactical devices, such as those advocated by Lenin to take advantage of the sentimental inhibitions of the apparently self-deluded "bourgeois."

In more sophisticated versions of modern—or rather postmodern—thought, the "fundamental" categories that I have called exoskeletal, are not, of course, primordial given things, but are themselves "cultural constructs." This seems to promise at least the possibility of *constructing* a common world of understanding, but in a frame of mind that posits the law of noncontradiction itself as arising from "construction" and thus subject to "deconstruction," given the absence of any possible reference to a formal scheme, much less to a reality transcending and thus validating the construct, it is hard to see why any two people would need to agree on any particular construct:

> "When *I* use a word," Humpty Dumpty said, in rather a scornful tone, "it means just what I choose it to mean—neither more nor less."
>
> "The question is," said Alice, "whether you *can* make words mean so many different things."

"The question is," said Humpty Dumpty, "which is to be master—that's all."[4]

Unmasking the game of power played with language must, it would seem, be itself a power game. All we can hope to do is avoid being deluded into slipping out of our carapace, which would make us easy prey "to those in power." We may miss the clarity of Marxist causalities of oppression, but dialectical mutations of "the Other" have not changed the Manichaean dualism in which, now this, now that identity seeks to be forged.

The attention paid to language, not only as a vehicle of notation and expression, but as itself a pattern that forms, and, to the extent that it can be manipulated, deforms thought, is well merited, and a familiar theme since George Orwell.[5] That what is said and thought about politics is not just an account of, but itself a constitutive part of the "effective reality of politics," we know since Machiavelli.[6] Karl Kraus showed how the style betrayed the author to an attentive ear and noted, in despair, that Hitler was beyond parody.[7] It is important that a liberal education awaken the students' awareness of the creative and, at the same time, potentially destructive power of language, and it must point to the fact that it is not just a mirror held up to a world of things that exist independently of it. The way in which we speak affects the way we think, not just the other way around. Some of our stereotypes are linguistic. The "Far East" expresses a very different perspective than the "Pacific Rim," the first measuring the world from Greenwich or Paris, the second informed by the experience and interests of late twentieth-century California. I cannot call a man "boy" and treat him like the man he is. A heightened sensitivity to the use of words, to their conditionality as an index of the conditionality of our understanding, is an excellent thing. But hermeneutic sensibility is frequently flattened to formulaic "causalities." It may well be that when we use "man" as the generic term for human being, we are inclined to think of men rather than women, of men as more fully human than women and thus subliminally reconfirm a sexist understanding of social relations. But this is a long way from structural determination. It is also true, conversely, that if I make a point of never using "man" to denote "human being" I *reduce* its meaning to signify "man as opposed to woman" *making* the word, in Humpty Dumpty's sense, mean less than it means, forcing a sexist reduction on it.

If we take the absence in English of a generic for human being, which is not identical with the word for the male of the species, as an effect of the culture's sexism, then we must assume that the English-speaking cultures are, in some significant respect, more sexist than cultures whose language, such as German or Greek, does distinguish between a man and a human being. This is, prima facie, an unlikely conclusion. The example does not prove, of course, that the English language does not reflect historically and socially internalized attitudes with regard to the relation of the sexes, only that evidence that is frequently adduced to that effect is inconclusive, because it is reductive and mechanical. The equally mechanical purported corrections are not only often clumsy— although that could, perhaps, be overcome with time—but seem hardly to the point. What is needed is a mastery of language, that is, a grasp of its force and of its ambiguities, not the turning of a few knobs. One cannot broaden the appeal and increase the strength of a justly cele- brated proclamation of universal importance by changing its wording to "The Rights of Person." Helping students develop a habit of think- ing of women and men when they think of "humanity" is entirely a good thing, but the most meticulous and tedious use of "she/he" will not prevent them from developing substantively sexist ideas and may, in fact, mislead them into thinking that that kind of tokenism is all it takes to overcome prejudice. The more absurd cases of changing evoca- tive *sounds* of words, regardless of etymology, in an attempt to over- come false consciousness, as in "herstory" for the study of the past from a female perspective, are again predicated on the presumption that the public is ignorant and is bound to remain so and is—much like refusing to wear fake furs because it might encourage those who can't tell the difference to wear real ones—a combination of self-righteous presumption and barbarism. But the widespread practice of mechani- cal "gender-neutrality" in writing,[8] is symptomatic of the superficiality that goes with wearing one's skeleton on the outside.

18

Herstory?

One of the side effects of racial nationalism and of analogous assertions of group solidarity—some versions of feminism in particular—has been the search for a cultural heritage specific to the group in question. The process is reminiscent of the romantic historiography and ethnography connected with the nineteenth-century awakening of European nationalism. Events of the past are interpreted and arranged, in what is often a fanciful play of fact and fiction, so as to provide a pedigree for the cultural unit as it is, or perhaps more eagerly, as it aspires to be. Elements of culture, works of art, ceremonial practices but also, and in particular, manifestations of everyday life, such as customs, costumes, fairy tales, the decorative arts, folk dances, are collected and cherished as emanations of the specific genius of the people, i.e., *this* people *as opposed* to *that* people, especially if that other people happens to be the one whose rule one wishes to shake off or simply one's neighbor and competitor whom one wishes to outshine.

These efforts, both in the nineteenth century and in our time, have brought to light and saved from oblivion a great many cultural manifestations and provided, as such, a valuable contribution to our civilizational horizon. Cultural expressions, retrieved and dusted off, can, when studied dispassionately, yield a wealth of insight into human creativity. To that extent, institutions devoted to such studies have much to offer to a general education.

On the whole, however, such institutions, the national museums of nineteenth-century Europe in their time and the Ethnic and Women's Studies centers now springing up all over American campuses, are not driven by a tender regard for what is specifically one's own or simply fragile and worth preserving or setting in a new light. They were and are driven by a search for ideological weapons by means of which to articulate and assert what is, at least on the surface, an uncertainly defined identity. Nationalist historiography must find, anachronistically, that Charlemagne was "really" French or "really" German, whereas, of course, he was neither, since he antedates the emergence of nationality in the modern sense. That does not mean that sensible continuities cannot be established, in terms of which one can give an intelligible account of events leading from Charlemagne to the French and the German present, respectively. But that is a matter of history, not of ideological appropriation of the past. And it is history, not ideology, that is a proper object of study in a liberal education.

Nationalist ethnography must find that a traditional piece of jewelry worn, say, in a village of northern Greece, which is, in fact, very similar to those worn in a Bulgarian village on the other side of the mountain, is "really" much more like the ones found on the purely Hellenic Aegean islands. A study of the actual spread of techniques or design patterns would have yielded more, if what one sought to understand were truly the character of artifacts, rather than the elusive soul of a people. The difficulty arises because ideological identity requires that everything that "belongs" be truly inside, and everything that does not be closed out. But that is not the way real people or real peoples live.

This kind of identity boosting requires a considerable degree of mental gymnastics. When the evidence, even under pressure, will not bear out the desired conclusion, it is a favorite device to proclaim that the pertinent evidence has been suppressed. The claim always has a degree of plausibility because, in the battle of identities evidence *does* get suppressed. One lot, having the upper hand, deliberately destroys vestiges of the existence of another in order to preempt possible claims in the name of the other. Sometimes, tragically, the vestiges destroyed are human communities. The ethnic Hungarian communities brutally uprooted by Romania's Ceausescu are a case in point.

But the alleged suppression of evidence is also an invitation to argue from silence, an invitation to invent a past in order to establish a present. "Writing one's own history" can mean asking questions of the evidence that others had no interest in exploring and perhaps even had an interest in suppressing. But it can also mean arranging what might count as evidence to suit one's ideological requirements. It is sometimes argued that history is never anything but this kind of self-serving arrangement, that all history is inevitably ideological. This, I think, is profoundly mistaken.

Although history, as the course of events, is open to interpretation, it is not a figment of the imagination. We all live in a world that has come about, and we are of this world whatever questions we may choose to ask about its emergence. We cannot choose to alter the manner in which it developed.

It is true that all societies seem to be held together in part by stories its people tell about their past and their origins. The way the stories are told tells us about the way people understand themselves in the present. The mythical part of the story is generally the most characteristic "historical" focus of a people's togetherness: for the Romans, the story from Romulus—or even Aeneas—to Tarquin; for Americans, Washington who "cannot tell a lie" or the Alamo as imagined. Some stories, the one about the Alamo for instance, need to be retold when the terms of togetherness change. Having lost its mythical aura, the story is, however, best retold in answer to historical, not mythical or countermythical questions. The myths that a society shares are not "unreal" because they are not positively factual, but their mode of reality is properly appreciated with a kind of detachment, such as that shown by Cicero's Scipio in *The Republic*. Viewed in this spirit they become meaningful points of reference without enslaving the mind.

It is again the business of a liberal education, not to seek to obliterate one myth with another, but to bring about this balanced detachment.

It is also an abuse of history when it is thought of as a gallery of glorious figures, vicariously reflecting on oneself. Naturally, a sense of continuity informs one's identity, and it can be a boost as much as a burden. Ancestor worship is deeply rooted in human nature, and it is understandable that people seek to establish an illustrious ancestry. By the same token, it is a cruel fate to have been uprooted and therefore unable to trace a meaningful line of descent. But everyone can relate, in principle, to great figures of the past in a broad range of human reference, that is, not genetically or even culturally determined. The answer to the exclusionary snobbery of "my ancestors sailed in the Mayflower" is "and mine sailed in Noah's Ark."

The psychologically reductive notion of "role model," which is so much in vogue, is much to blame for the need to establish an exoskeletal past of one's own. It is not easy to "find oneself" in terms of universal humanity, but there is also something unseemly about scrambling to show that "my ancestors were as good or better than yours." "Was Cleopatra Black?" on the cover of *Time* magazine, shows the absurdities of fact to which such a scramble can lead.[1] But what is worse, it adopts the frivolous vanity that a human being, whose nation, race, or family never accomplished anything notable at all, should command for that reason less respect than a fellow creature, created like all human beings in the Creator's image.

19

Conformity and Individuality

The lure of power and public recognition held out by exoskeletal group solidarity has also attracted adherents whose proclaimed identity would seem to be quintessentially individual, thus creating a paradox. Self-enactment, though never exactly a *creatio ex nihilo,* since, like all performances, it requires an audience, is typically an individual, not a collective accomplishment.

There is no reason why a liberal order should object to self-enacted identities, no matter how eccentric, as long as the conduct they imply does not violate the principle of reciprocity; as long, that is, as others are not hindered in the pursuit, subject to the same limitation, of *their* good as they see it. Surely, if the "pursuit of happiness," to which we are held to have an inalienable right, doesn't just mean the ability to make money, it must mean something like that.

Describing the vibrantly diverse Alexandria before the nationalist revival in Egypt leveled it out, Lawrence Durrell writes, "Five races, five languages, a dozen creeds: five fleets turning through their greasy reflections behind the harbour bar. But there are more than five sexes and only demotic Greek seems to distinguish among them."[1] Memberships in the collective entities—race, language, creed—sometimes run together, sometimes crisscross as do the allegiances, given, opportunistic or imposed, to one or more of the fleets in the harbor. But why would people whose identity was marked by many other things besides, and then showed a great variety of sexual inclinations, want to be put into the straightjacket of a common "lifestyle"?

The reason is, I think, that, as John Stuart Mill pointed out, in a conformist society, "the man, and still more the woman, who can be accused either of doing 'what nobody does' or of not doing 'what everybody does,' is the subject of as much depreciatory remark as if he or she had committed some grave moral delinquency."[2]

On the model of religious toleration, Mill argues, only such tastes and modes of life are tolerated by the law and, more importantly, by public opinion, as "extort acquiescence by the multitude of their adherents." Departures from uniformity incur blame unless "both those who like each of [a variety of activities] and those who dislike them, are too numerous to be put down." The pressures of conformity are especially great in democratic societies, because practices diverging from those of the greater number cannot be considered peculiar to people who stick out in some other, commonly accepted way. Yet diversity is essential, because

> such are the differences among human beings in their sources of pleasure, their susceptibilities of pain, and the operation on them of different physical and moral agencies, that unless there is a corresponding diversity in their modes of life, they neither obtain their fair share of happiness, nor grow up to the mental, moral and aesthetic stature of which their nature is capable.[3]

In an egalitarian society, in which "the very idea of resisting the will of the public disappears," the pressures of conformity lead those who wish to depart from it to adopt its modes even as they seek to oppose it. Nonconformity itself appears in the form of a secondary conformity, in the adoption and proclamation of formulaic "lifestyles."

It has become fashionable to decry individuality as both selfish and illusory and to conceive diversity not as the freedom and variety of situations necessary for individual human development, but as the collective manifestations of racial, sexual, economic, and other exoskeletal determinations. That human individuality needs to struggle against formidable pressures is undeniable, but pressures are not determinations. If human consciousness were truly determined, it could not be controlled one way or the other by deliberate action. If, on the other hand, it is taken to be the result of manipulation by the powers that be, then the manipulation can be unmasked and undone.

A trick that is seen to be a trick no longer works. If the "secrets of power" are common knowledge, they are ineffective. The generic vagueness with which the alleged causes of distortion and subjugation are described—"the overall operation of the established forces in the society," for example, constituting "institutional" as opposed to "individual" racism, according to Stokely Carmichael—make it impossible to identify, and hence to oppose any particular instances or agents of domination, leaving as possible responses only the hope of metastatic change or defeatism and despair. This does not prevent intellectuals from arrogating to themselves, in the same miraculous manner of Lenin's unlamented "avant-garde," the capacity to penetrate the fog of our false consciousness, escaping the determinations of social and cultural power by recognizing it (according to their lights) for what it is. That, some teachers of humanities maintain, is the very mark of their professional calling, what distinguishes them from "amateurs—belle-lettrists who unself-consciously sustain traditional hierarchies, traditional social and cultural exclusions, assuming that their audience is both universal and homogeneous."[4]

What is presented as exclusionary is the assumption of a modicum of common humanity in one's potential audience. In order not to falsify his message, the professor of anthropology must deliver his lecture about the Hopi in Hopi. Authors who "write from their own experience" (how else?) must, we are compelled to infer, seek a *specialized* audience, one, presumably, which already shares that experience, instead of being deluded into thinking that their works might be understood by human beings as such. A reviewer of books by and about women asks, "What is experience: not imagination, friendships, dreams, reading"? And further, in response to dynamic efforts of women "to write themselves" into the culture: "Why is it that groups formed by people with similar stories in order to overcome oppression, isolation, and silencing and to recognize their special values as a community so often breed a group mind that begins patrolling the borders?"[5]

The common humanity of diverse human beings, renamed "homogeneity," is split up by the guardians of the new orthodoxy into particularized, self-referential audiences. The rounded, educated human being, the traditional aim of a liberal education, is an "amateur," the dupe of "hegemonic discourse" and illusory "Eurocentric" values. It is professional specialization, we learn, that can master the lobster pond of redefined "discourses," even as it guards against the transmission of "traditional hierarchies," defining what is admissible in culture and what is not. In such a scheme of professional service to—or, should one say, mastery of—partial, self-regarding, yet always collective uniformities, a liberal education has no place:

> it is not by wearing down into uniformity all that is individual in themselves, but by cultivating it, and calling it forth, within the limits imposed by the rights and interests of others, that human beings become a noble and beautiful object of contemplation; and as the works partake the character of those who do them, by the same process human life also becomes rich, diversified, and animating, furnishing more abundant aliment to high thoughts and elevating feelings, and strengthening the tie which binds every individual to the race, by making the race infinitely better worth belonging to.[6]

Part 3

The Confusion of Tongues

20

What Is the Tower of Babel For?

One technological society is not like another. There is much to choose from between societies whose citizens enjoy political liberties and individual rights and those where that is not the case. A Marcuse may claim that the "one-dimensional" America he fled to is as bad or worse than the Germany he left behind, but we may well have reason to doubt that. Free societies also seem to be more efficient, but this is not the main reason for preferring them, for freedom is worth having, even if one has to do with less. Having said that, freedom from hunger and misery, the control of disease, the everyday amenities of life are all goods and necessary, though admittedly not sufficient, conditions for a fuller unfolding of human creativity. No society is *merely* technological, and the degree of play that each society enjoys with regard to its functional needs narrowly understood, is quite considerable. But there is no denying the leveling pressures of technology and organizational rationality. The variety of situations, and hence of liberty itself, which are the conditions of individuality, are threatened by the conformist complacency of material contentment and the inexorable rise of a bureaucratic-legal order. Technological societies *are* alike, in important respects, and in these respects difference between private and public ownership of the apparatus of production is not what is decisive. The playwright and first president of free Czechoslovakia and now of the Czech Republic, Václav Havel, having described the appalling effects of the command economy under his country's communist regime on the creativity and humanity of its people, continued,

> Enormous private multinational corporations are curiously like socialist states; with industrialization, centralization, specialization, monopolization, and finally with automation and computerization, the elements of depersonalization and the loss of meaning in work becomes more and more profound everywhere. Along with that goes the general manipulation of peoples' lives by the system (no matter how inconspicuous such manipulation may be, compared with that of the totalitarian state). IBM certainly works better than the Skoda plant, but that doesn't alter the

fact that both companies have long since lost their human dimension and have turned man into a little cog in their machinery, utterly separated from what, and for whom, that machinery is working.[1]

Unleavened by individuality, frantic activity, pursued automatically, but conceived as a duty, has no visible links to spiritual and cultural values. "The Puritan wanted to work in a calling," states Max Weber, "we are forced to do so."[2] The modern "rationally" administered world becomes "an iron cage": "Specialists without spirit, sensualists without heart; this nullity imagines that it has attained a level of civilization never before achieved."[3]

Unexamined, the titanic effort of modernity is building a monument to vainglory. As in Brueghel's famous picture, even as the colossal tower reaches upward, dwarfing nature and the older structures that were in the measure of man, the foundations are in need of repair. What, we ask again, is the Tower of Babel for?

The disillusion with the modern project is all the greater because its promise was so grand.[4] The collective self-determination of mankind, the complete mastery of nature, is limited by the fallibility of man, manifest in the "confusion of tongues." The enterprise in its pride risks becoming a spiritual disaster, even if it doesn't lead to physical catastrophe. The effort of man to make himself divine is folly.

More modestly, the realization that scientific and technical knowledge, taken by itself, is morally inert and, in its very universality, humanly colorless and anonymous, awakens the thirst for knowledge of a different kind. Beyond the pressures, connected with having to bake an ever-bigger pie to keep everyone quiet, human freedom, the yearning for meaning, the quest for identity, assert themselves.

> The greatest drawback of our educational methods, is that we pay an excessive amount of attention to the natural sciences and not enough to ethics. Our chief fault is that we disregard that part of ethics which treats of human character, of its dispositions, its passions and of the manner of adjusting these factors to public life and the ability to speak well. We neglect that discipline which deals with the differential features of the virtues and vices, with good and bad behavior patterns, with the typical characteristics of the old and the young, of the two sexes, of social and economic class, race and nation, and with the art of seemly conduct in life, the most difficult of all arts. . . . Since in our time, the only target of our intellectual endeavors is scientific truth, we devote all our efforts to the investigation of physical phenomena, because their nature seems unambiguous; but we fail to inquire into human nature which, because of the freedom of man's will, is difficult to determine. . . . Our young peo-

ple, because of their training, which is focused on these studies, are unable to engage in the life of the community, to conduct themselves with sufficient wisdom and good sense. Their speech lacks familiarity with human psychology and their utterances lack verve.[5]

The situation described seems familiar enough, but it is hardly new. This text was produced by Giambattista Vico in early eighteenth-century Naples. Clearly, more is involved than a current crisis. The tensions and incongruities that we have become so acutely aware of are, it seems, inherent in the principles of understanding characteristic of the modern world.

Many people today, it is true, would prefer to see greater attention to ethics *and* as much if not more science taught to the young. When asked how and when this could be done, they point to the sorry state of elementary and secondary schools and the time, energy, and goodwill that is wasted there. But the text I quoted could be a fair expression of contemporary preoccupation with education as it concerns the realm of values, of ethical choice and political involvement. It could well have been part of a brief presented to the MIT planning committee of what has now become the Alfred P. Sloan School of Management.[6] The problem arises from the conflict between the nature of scientific knowledge—impersonal and morally inert—on the one hand, and the personal nature of moral freedom, of prudent judgment and of what, for lack of a better word, might be called social skills, on the other. Vico had clearly recognized the cognitive problems long before, in the face of the momentous transformation effected by industrial society, C. P. Snow sought to capture its sociological manifestations in *The Two Cultures*.[7]

21

A Scientific Morality?

Despite Vico's warnings, science came to be identified by some of its practitioners and would-be practitioners with knowledge itself. It came to be seen not as one possible mode of knowledge, appropriate to certain fields and patterns of cognition, but as the only manner of real knowledge, guaranteeing its own validity.[1]

"I believe," wrote Linus Pauling, "that it is possible to formulate a fundamental principle of morality, independent of revelation, superstition, dogma, and creed and acceptable by all human beings in a scientific, rational way by analyzing the facts presented to us by the evidence of our senses."[2]

The Nobel Prize–winning scientist relegates what cannot be established scientifically to the realm of superstition and its more elevated religious equivalents. Morality can be determined by the rational analysis of empirical evidence: "I hurt like the next man, hence I recognize that I am like the next man." One might object, of course, that I have no sense experience of how the next man hurts, for it is he, not I, who hurts when he hurts. I can only infer that he hurts like I do, because I somehow know that he is like me, and *therefore* his hurt must be like mine. I recognize him as a man (like me) before I can identify his pain with mine, and it is the recognition of common humanity that yields the notion of community of pain, not vice versa. It is a petition of principle. Pain can, of course, be the starting point for a moral theory. Bentham, for instance, pointed out that in order to decide whether a creature has rights, the pertinent question is not whether it is capable of reason, but whether it is capable of suffering. But Bentham developed this thought in order to establish the rights of *animals,* that is, not in order to delimit humanity in its specificity, but in order to extend our moral obligation beyond the human community. Pauling's "empirical" foundation of *human* community on suffering opens the door not to all men but to a whole zoo.

The next step establishes, according to this world-famous and well-meaning man, the equality of men. "Now my observation leads me to believe that there is nothing special about me that sets me apart from other human beings in any fundamental way."

Give or take two Nobel Prizes, there is nothing to set off Pauling from the next Joe Blow. But maybe that is not a "fundamental" difference. What makes a difference "fundamental," however, clearly does not result from observation. Observation can only confirm or falsify whether a distinction I have *already* recognized as fundamental is present, assuming that the presumed fundamental distinction is of the observable kind.

From such premises, Pauling derives a universal law, capable of transcending all cultures and establishing the foundation of a world without war:

> I want to be free of suffering to the greatest extent possible. I want to live a happy and useful life, a satisfying life.

Let us assume we know what it means to lead a happy life and that it is clear what utility is served in a "satisfying" life.

> I want other people to help me to be happy, to help me to keep my suffering to a minimum. It is accordingly my duty to help them to be happy, to strive to prevent suffering from other people.

My desire to be helped by others hardly establishes my obligation to help them *unless* I have already postulated the rule of reciprocity, which is not an empirical datum. In the absence of reciprocity I may be better served by slaves. Notice, in any case, that for Pauling the desire for happiness is prior and determines the sense of duty, a doctrine which, though quite familiar in the modern West, would certainly puzzle a great many people living by other codes in East and West alike. "By this argument, I am led to a fundamental ethical principle that decisions among alternative courses of action should be made in such ways as to minimize the predicted amount of suffering."

QED. Science can provide a calculus of suffering, indeed of expected *future* suffering, e.g., mental anguish, 3; leg amputated, 2; sweetheart killed, 4. . . .

Armed with this scientific morality, Pauling feels "forced" by "the greatly increased understanding of the nature of the world and the tremendous technological development to which it has led . . . to become involved in politics." Yet, "the politicians and national leaders have not yet called upon the scientists for help in analyzing the extremely complex problems that must be solved if war is to be abolished and replaced by world law based upon an ethical principle and in searching for acceptable and practical solutions to these problems."

Congress, recognizing the weakness of decision makers chosen for reasons other than their scientific and technical expertise in assessing technological questions has in fact taken steps to correct this weakness. It has, for instance, enlisted the cooperation of the American Association for the Advancement of Science, setting up the Congressional Fellows program, under which qualified scientists spend a year working as legislative advisors—and in some cases stay on to make careers of it. It has created the Office of Technology Assessment, an extremely important and successful agency which does studies for Congress on technological issues so that Congress does not have to depend only on the advice it gets from promoters of technology in the executive departments and the private sector.[3] Congress's action in this regard quite properly distinguishes between competent technical advice and political responsibility, but this is precisely the line that Pauling refuses to draw. Pauling accordingly laments that there are no scientists in Congress, although many of its deliberations relate to science. Scientists (qua scientists) should, in his view, not only advise but actually make the decisions themselves. Nevertheless, forced as he feels to participate in politics, waiting to be called upon by national leaders, he cannot subdue his abhorrence of politics: "I fear that the training of a scientist, the inculcation of the sort of morality that lies at the basis of all science, respect for the truth, unfits him to serve in Congress."

Pauling, convinced there is a simple, self-evident, or anyway scientifically identifiable common goal for humanity, has no patience with the knitting together of incommensurable interests and points of view. Political accommodation amounts to corruption. The Greens in Germany, who also know themselves in possession of an unequivocal truth, express a similar antipolitical self-righteousness by means of a pithy slogan: "Wahrheit nicht Mehrheit"—"Truth, not majority." For Pauling, if you don't "think like a scientist," that is, act in the conviction that in all matters you can arrive by unerring methods from assured premises to indisputable conclusions, you are a crook.

It has become commonplace to deplore the absence of scientific and technical understanding in governing elites and, indeed, under the imperative of democratic self-government, in the general population. In a technological age, we read in countless newspaper and magazine articles that citizens must be technologically literate. A fortiori, political representatives ought to be able to evaluate matters of public policy that these days inevitably bear on technical matters, often involving great risk and expense.

It is doubtful that a smattering of applied physics and chemistry at school, or even at university, will enable the public and its chosen representatives to make up their own minds on technical projects brought before them without expert advice. C. P. Snow, not so long ago, wanted everyone to know at least the Second Law of Thermodynamics. The truth is that we now need to understand the principles of molecular biology a lot more than we need to understand that law of physics. Even so, the chances that even the best-informed layman will be able to keep up with the next frontier of scientific discovery are extremely slim. Trying to make everyone an omnicompetent expert is an absurdity. But it is quite conceivable that the capacity of a significant number of significantly placed people to tell good advice from bad can be vastly improved. What is needed for that is not the command of a vast amount of information, for there would never be enough of that, and even specialists have trouble keeping up with developments in their respective fields. What is required is, rather, a particular manner of critical thought, an understanding of the nature of scientific judgment. A familiarity with the manner in which science is done would, therefore, be a valuable part of anyone's education. But an informed critical competence is not, in itself, a scientific finding.

A familiarity with the nature of scientific evidence would, furthermore, help contain the excessive reliance on science, the aping of its methods in fields to which they are not suited and limit the blind confidence in its capacity to deliver certitudes. That would be beneficial not only in abating an easy optimism leading to possibly irresponsible decisions—e.g., "they will find a way to dispose of nuclear waste before it becomes a problem"—but also serve as a guard against pessimism when such hopes are deluded. When science is seen to be flawed, as at some point it must—in a false diagnosis, for example—the entire edifice can be called into question, opening the door to every conceivable irrationalism. It is not that there is no such thing as malpractice, but many suits are brought and decided on the notion that a doctor can act on something more certain than his best considered opinion.

In a technological age, many decisions of public concern require technical expertise. That is, in fact, true even at a relatively low level of technical development. It was a technical question for the ancient Athenians, for instance, whether the navigating and strategic advantages of a trireme, a warship with three rows of oars, for example, over a lighter craft, justified the additional expense. But decisions, though best taken in the light of competent technical advice, are, in the end, political decisions. Take the recent flurry of activity over asbestos, for example. Quite apart from the technical blunder of causing more of the stuff to fly around in the process of removing it than would ever have been the case had it been left where it was, the question was not how to remove a source of certain damage to the public, but, rather, what degree of possible danger was tolerable, measured against the costs of eliminating it. This is not unlike the possible danger of using the public roads. The choice of what risk is acceptable, all things considered, is not technical, but political. Pauling's "scientific" formula of "minimizing suffering" offers little guidance.

It is true that very few scientists and engineers are elected or appointed to public office. It is no doubt the case that they are hindered in doing so by the nature of their training. If they were more articulate, that is, in Snow's terms sufficiently trained in literary culture, and if they made less of a virtue of being taciturn, they could come forward not only as expert advisors, but as decision makers and opinion leaders.[4] But in a sense, the inner reluctance that Pauling spoke of is perhaps a greater impediment. It is tempting to tell yourself that you are taking the high ground when choosing to stay aloof from the rough and tumble of public life, as it is to dismiss what is not amenable to scientific and technical reasoning as being beyond reason. Engineers resent being ruled by lawyers—and in business by money-men—but they are on the whole reluctant to come forward themselves. Naturally, in a society that lives by rules and that values expertise, the experts on rules, lawyers, will be in charge of developing and applying rules. Since rules are necessary, because of the imperfection of mankind, lawyers are both needed and resented. Only when it is recognized that, at the highest level, the rules that hold society together are not the subject of a particular expertise, and that the rounded human being is not one who has simply added this expertise to that, that lawyers can be put in their place. There is always enough corruption and folly in the way human beings conduct their affairs to serve as an excuse, in the high name of science, or purity of heart, to stay aloof. The refusal to "dirty one's hands" with politics can, however, also be seen as an abdication, an act of cowardice, and a dereliction of duty.

Pauling, as we saw, experiences the "two cultures" as a division between an obscurantist, corrupt, or foolish part of humanity, including most politicians, and an enlightened part, capable of transforming all aspects of the human predicament, moral, political, and technical, into problems similar to the problems of science. The unity, according to him, should be accomplished in the mode of science, tendentially abolishing politics in the name of "problem solving," that is transforming the government of men, as Saint-Simon intended, into the administration of things.

It would be grossly unfair to Pauling to say that he ever advocated violence, except perhaps by omission.[5] But the frame of mind he advances has a natural appeal to more forceful modernizers, frequently but not always military men who seek to eradicate the ills of society by sweeping politics aside. What is intellectually ambiguous, i.e., open to deliberation, is declared morally shady in the name of more or less high-sounding certitudes, which are duly imposed with results that have become altogether too familiar in our century.

A variation of the scientistic ideal, managerialism, i.e., the idea that a country ought to be run like a business, and that, therefore, a successful businessman is best qualified to lead it, has also found broad popular support.[6] In the midst of populist antipolitical enthusiasm it is easily forgotten that the life of a country is not summed up by a bottom line.

22

Two Cultures?

In his celebrated essay, C. P. Snow also approaches the divide from the side of science. He distinguishes between a "literary" and a "scientific" culture, but whereas the latter remains rather precisely defined, the former is soon identified with "traditional" culture and finally becomes a residual category covering "non-scientists." The line is drawn by science. To be sure, Snow deplores the division itself, and he points to the drawbacks for society (or at least for the part of society that engages in conversation) and for the individuals in question, of the lack of a literary education characteristic of the scientific community. His main concern, however, is with the "total incomprehension of science" on the part of those he calls "literary intellectuals."[1]

A general education, he argues, should encompass both, but, in the manner of a scientist, his titles as a novelist notwithstanding, he treats the two sides of the divide as different but equivalent fields of knowledge, rather than as distinct modes of understanding. It is all in the mode of "knowing about": some people know about Shakespeare, others know about thermodynamics. It is unfortunate that those who know about the one are ignorant about the other. But in principle the two groups differ only by having command over a different body of information. What drives Snow's argument is the proposition that "industrialization is the only hope of the poor," in both industrialized societies and developing countries.[2] What such countries need is not the paternalism of Jesuit or Protestant missionaries, but "men who will muck in as colleagues, who will pass on what they know, do an honest technical job and get out. Fortunately, this is an attitude which comes easily to scientists."[3] Snow is undoubtedly right in thinking that, whatever other drawbacks it may have, industrialization is the only way out of poverty. It provides the material conditions of mobility for individuals and entire peoples alike. There can be no doubt that what all underdeveloped countries want from the West, however opposed they may be to its social, political, and religious values, is its technology as the indispensable means to affluence and, a matter not mentioned by

Snow, in most cases, the perceived advantages, material and moral, of efficient, that is, modern, technically equipped, and rationally organized military power.

Looking back over three decades since Snow delivered his Rede Lecture, one can see that technical and economic development has been very uneven among the several developing countries, as has been the distribution of relative benefits and power among different strata within the several developing societies, giving in many cases as much cause for despair as for hope. Prosperity itself, where it has been achieved, has brought its own problems. It is, in any case, far from clear that the transmission of organizational skills and technical transfers could be effected quite as impersonally as Snow's outline would suggest. Some cultures and some personalities are better suited to the acquisition of certain skills, and all go through pains of transition. The same view of depersonalized communication as the sharing of information characterizes Snow's view of the desired relationship between the "two cultures" in developed societies as well. Arguing in the context of a society still largely ruled by the "literary" or "traditionally educated," he seeks to demonstrate the importance and the dignity of science.[4] Rutherford, he writes, was "absolutely right" to cast himself as the Shakespeare of the new Elizabethan age, the heroic age of science.[5] To admit without blushing that one doesn't know the Second Law of Thermodynamics is the equivalent of saying that one has not read a single work by Shakespeare.[6] It is, of course, foolish to underestimate the importance of science in modern life and presumptuous to give oneself airs of superiority with regard to its practitioners, whose "intensive, rigorous culture . . . contains a great deal of argument, usually much more rigorous," as Snow quite rightly points out and, somewhat more controversially, "almost always at a higher conceptual level than literary persons' arguments."[7] It is always better to know things than not to know them and better to know more rather than less. But a cultivated human being is not a larger receptacle of information than a less cultivated human being. He is, rather, someone who has been formed by creative responses to manifestations of civilization, one who has integrated the vicarious experience of reading, for instance, into a personality that is different, fuller than it was before. Science can do this, no doubt, to the extent that it is experienced as an intellectual adventure, but at the level of rules and applicable results like the Second Law of Thermodynamics it is just information, of as much or as little formative value as knowing the height of Mount Everest. It is to say that science is cumulative, and one can be a dwarf on the shoulders of giants but nonetheless a dwarf.

Literature, on the other hand, or art, or philosophy, lives in the recreative response of the reader or observer, who does not simply acquire a new possession, but is changed by responding. One's experience of it is personal or it is nothing. Snow is, of course, sensitive to the personal core of experience and hence of education: "The individual condition of each of us is tragic. Each of us is alone: sometimes we escape from solitariness, through love or attention or perhaps creative moments, but those triumphs of life are pools of light we make for ourselves while the edge of the road is black: each of us dies alone."[8]

Snow is sensitive to the personal, but he is reductive. He is quick to flee the loneliness of the individual condition drawn by the promise held out by collective social progress. What such progress means is taken to be self-evident. To the extent that science offers to be a mechanism conducive to the latter, it is a welcome cause for optimism and an essential corrective against the temptation "to sit back, complacent in one's unique tragedy, and let the other go without a meal."[9] In a familiar pattern, Snow's science allows one to fulfill one's duty by doing one's appointed task, putting one's shoulder to the wheel of collective progress, providing universal Meals on Wheels.

But the individuality of human creativity beyond our separate and yet universal mortality is not loneliness, but the very foundation of genuine sociability. What is shared is personal, which is why sharing it is meaningful. That is what a culture is. Although it creates a common world, it is not "out there," like a public park or a multiplication table, neither mine nor thine, there for all to use or leave alone. The privileged vehicle of culture is conversation. Conversation is about something, of course, but it engages the persons of the interlocutors. It is not a mutual debriefing.

The elements of a literary culture evoke personal responses. In this it is more like everyday life than any professional specialty. This is why a doctor, a lawyer, and an engineer can have a conversation about *The Tempest,* (or a football game) but can only inform each other about vaccines, torts, and fluid mechanics, respectively. When people have no more to share than their respective expertise, they no longer meet like people, but like members of a committee.[10]

"The scientific culture," Snow writes, "really is a culture, not only in the intellectual but also in the anthropological sense . . . there are common attitudes, common standards and patterns of behavior, common approaches and assumptions . . . without thinking about it, they respond alike. That is what a culture means."[11]

If culture really means a set of conditioned reflexes, even if it be thought to drive the wheel of universal progress (how would one know?), I doubt that any civilized human being would want any part of it. Surely what is needed is the *thoughtful* integration of the different modes of human understanding. It is because minds can meet, by means of words, that science, among other things, is possible.

23

The Retreat from the Word

Vico lamented the loss of ethical reflection and the retreat of language before the advance of science. In fact, the triumphant march of technology has left us speechless. Its very success has made the manner of knowledge that underpins it the paradigm of all trustworthy knowledge. But it is a knowledge increasingly inexpressible in words. The formally coherent logical space that it demands which, along with empirical verification, establishes its validity, rejects the ambiguities of natural language. The abstract mathematical notation that it requires and develops becomes increasingly divorced from the world of everyday experience. It acquires a life of its own, for which it becomes impossible to find verbal equivalents. Euclidean geometry was, of course, already a highly formalized language, relying in great part on nonverbal forms of abstraction. But just as Euclid's abstractions appeared to fit and measure the world of commonsense experience, it also seemed possible, however imperfectly, to put that which his abstraction signified into so many words. By contrast, the powerful symbolic languages invented since Descartes and Leibnitz create a world apart, accessible, of course, to those conversant with its notation but incommunicable in real language, literally unspeakable.[1] There is a double irony in this process: 1) the more powerful the intervention of man into nature became, the more abstract and further removed from commonsense experience became the reasoning behind it; 2) the more logically unified the world of natural science aimed to be, the more splintered became the notational languages of its practitioners. The curious result is that the loss of language not only divorced technical/scientific/mathematical culture, from humanistic/verbal culture, but it came to impede communication within technical culture itself.

   J. Robert Oppenheimer regarded the problem of splintering specializations as fundamental and insuperable. He thought it impossible to explain the concepts of modern mathematics and physics to the man in the street without distorting them. The misunderstandings combined with the illusion of understanding do more harm than good. "What is needed . . . is a harsh modesty, an affirmation that common men cannot, in fact, understand most things and that the realities of which even a highly trained intellect has cognizance are few and far between."[2]

Others are more optimistic and prefer to attribute the absence of unifying pictures of science and of its place in the natural and social world to deficient pedagogical practices. Thus, in a recent report entitled *The Liberal Arts and Science: Agenda for Action,* the American Association for the Advancement of Science notes:

> Traditional courses . . . often leave the students with incomplete or incorrect knowledge of scientific principles, underdeveloped intellectual skills and little awareness of the influence of science on their lives.

What they propose as a remedy amounts to a return to the word:

> Treat education in Natural Science as a liberal art . . . integrated into the general education curriculum. Subject matter must be broadened to encompass aspects of the history, philosophy, sociology and economics of science and technology.[3]

Who would have thought that mathematics, that noble edifice of unambiguous clarity and coherence would be transformed, at least for the great mass of undergraduates, into a Tower of Babel? We witness the Association for the Advancement of *Science* pleading for verbal communication. Understanding of the principles of science must pass, it says, not by entering directly into the uncontaminated sphere of mathematical form or the unimpeded observation of pristine nature, but first by way of a familiarity with the contingent, changeable, messy circumstances of human society, of economics, history, politics, and the rest of it. It would seem that unimpeded observation of a candid material world, heightened by abstraction and leading to ingenious applications, a manner of thinking to which we owe the spectacular success of technical achievement, is in its purity too good to be true. It must, it would seem, look back to its human, historical, social conditions of possibility and can only reveal itself in ordinary language, with all the imperfections and ambiguities that this entails.

But exactly how will "natural science as a liberal art" be "integrated into the general education curriculum"? "Integrated" is a carefully chosen word. It leaves open the question of whether the courses now constituting general education curricula would be supplemented by new courses, adapted, or dropped to make room for the new requirements. Clearly the association wants to do something innovative, going beyond "traditional courses." In the end, however, it seems to follow the most common response to changing educational and social needs and pressures, which is to "broaden the curriculum," rather than to rethink and restructure the educational offerings. One needs to wonder, with an eye to the finite time at the disposal of any student, whether the history, philosophy, sociology, and economics of science and technology will be studied as well as or instead of history, philosophy, sociology, and economics proper. How much of each can be done with any seriousness?

We encounter the limits of the attempt to bring about a universality of understanding by trying to "cover the ground." The attempt to prepare young people to meet the endless contingencies of life by trying to exhaust the list of possible contingencies is futile. However long the list of items in which instruction should be given, the list will never be complete. Reality does not consist of finite, determinate entities that, if we lack the intellectual courage to classify, we might be content to enumerate.

> So long as we conceive intellectual education as merely consisting in the acquirement of mechanical mental aptitudes, and of formulated statements of useful truth, there can be no progress; though there will be much activity, amid aimless re-arrangement of syllabuses, in the fruitless endeavour to dodge the inevitable lack of time. We must take it as an unavoidable fact that God has so made the world that there are more topics desirable for knowledge than any one person can possibly acquire. It is hopeless to approach the problem by the way of the enumeration of subjects which everyone ought to have mastered.[4]

This ever-popular Sisyphian project of complete enumeration is but a prolongation of the widespread misconception that knowledge is primarily a matter of registering and filing away facts, as though facts were given and did not need to be established. The vision of a coherent world of thought emerging as an accurate reflection of a coherent world of (given) things is very reassuring: but it is, of course, neither scientific nor humane.

The naturalist illusion claims to offer objectifiable criteria of validation, such as formal coherence and empirical verification, which neither require nor permit personal judgment. The mind is thought to register—like a photographic plate—the stuff that is out there. This kind of knowledge does not need a personal center to integrate its various facets. It is independent of the personal qualities of the knower. This is also why it can be taught impersonally. It is, exactly, textbook knowledge. It fits the pattern of instrumental knowledge.

What textbooks convey is a knowledge of what has been authoritatively said, not a familiarity with the way of thinking that gave rise to what was said.[5] They are best suited to vocational training, by which I mean as much the vocational training of an historian or an Egyptologist as that of a civil engineer or of a nurse; a training that requires the acquisition of a discrete, circumscribed body of knowledge—for it is not primarily the subject matter that makes an education or any part of it liberal or vocational.[6] The textbook, then, if it is up to date, will convey the "state of the art." It will communicate what is thought to be the state of knowledge by the reputed authorities in each field. The diligent student will learn to find his way around this body of information and so develop skills, which will, no doubt, be further developed by practice.

None of this is to be despised, for we all depend on skilled practitioners of various disciplines and trades. The greatest drawback of vocational training as a complete education is that it aims at the product, not at the producer. The formation of the professional is incidental to the exercise of the profession. It is intended as a mechanism for generating "human resources." Seen in this instrumental perspective alone, human beings, however admired, lucrative or otherwise exalted their vocation may be, are means, and not ends, and in this sense they are unfree.

Instrumental knowledge, aiming at what is done rather than at the manner of person who does it, can, in fact, dispense with people altogether. It can be externalized and registered in a machine. Spellcheckers are a simple example of this: the person who runs a text through the spellchecker comes up with a product free of spelling errors but remains for all that as ignorant as before. Indeed, a robot would do a better job.[7] This is, of course, one of the charms of the computer: by removing the need to do tedious and time-consuming mechanical work, and by doing it better, it liberates the thinking person—that is, one who can already think—to do creative work. Whether one is a master of the machine or its slave will depend on one's intellectual formation, on one's education, and that the machine cannot replace.

The bridge between the cultures will not be built by adding chapters to extant textbooks, nor even by bringing stuff together in some comprehensive, "interdisciplinary" supertextbook.

The gap between cultures, be there two or more, can only be bridged by recovering language, seeking to translate from one idiom to another, knowing full well that every translation is also a betrayal, but much less so when we are aware that this is so. We have to come to terms with the fracturing of cognitive specialties. The rifts cannot be mended by a universal science or some future generation of computers and certainly not by a couple of extra physics classes at high school—useful as these would be. They can only be mended by human community, which is, when it reasons, a community of speech.

Yet the word is retreating from the very area of human life where it should be most at home. Television, for example, hailed with some justification as a significant factor in the liberation of Eastern Europe, is, of course, a major force in electoral politics. During the U.S. election campaign of 1968, from Labor Day to Election Day the average "sound bite" granted the presidential candidates on weekday evening newscasts, the average unit of time when the audience actually got to hear the candidates speak, was 42.3 seconds. By 1988 this time had been reduced to 9.8 seconds! The time devoted to images, on the other hand, so-called "visuals" of the candidates, increased by more than 300 percent.[8]

English is a rich language said to contain some six hundred thousand words or one hundred times as many as there are in the King James version of the Bible. But 50 percent of colloquial English consists of no more than thirty-four basic words.

> To make themselves widely understood contemporary media of mass communication have to reduce English to a semiliterate condition. . . . The writer of today tends to use far fewer simple words, both because mass culture has watered down the concept of literacy and because the sum of realities of which words can give a necessary and sufficient account has sharply diminished.[9]

Schoolbooks are run through a computer by their publishers, with the approval, if not at the insistence, of the committees who select them, to make sure they contain no words that are too long or difficult. The books then talk down to the students, giving them no opportunity to stretch and grow and open windows to the world as only words can. In an eighth grade "social studies" manual used by the School District of San Diego, California, the word *redemptive* is explained away in a footnote to the "I Have a Dream" speech of Martin Luther King for fear perhaps that the student may stop and seek to bend back the unfamiliar word into the context and make it come alive and, thus, not only expand his vocabulary but quicken his sensibility to a way of looking at the world marked by King's spirituality, and the tradition in which it lives. To bring things down to what the committee—or the computer—thinks is the child's level is to betray the child's trust. The point is not to squeeze stuff within a static linguistic horizon, but to move the horizon itself. In this sense, kids should always be given readings that are "above their heads."

The *word*—articulate, differentiated speech—is everywhere in retreat and most ominously so in politics. The memorable reduction of Walter Mondale's message to the three syllables, "Where's the beef?" was destined to be outdone in due course by the persuasive silence of Willie Horton's picture.

24

Teaching Values

From the point of view of the educational planner, vocational education has the enormous advantage of being clear about its aims. He knows what end product he wishes to obtain, and he adopts the means most suitable to attaining the desired result. One may study law or medicine without wishing to practice either, but to become a lawyer or a physician, one *must* study law or medicine, respectively. But one does not become a statesman by studying political science or a man of the world by studying geography. The most laborious study of philosophy provides no sure path to wisdom, and it is difficult to imagine a course capable of building character. In the realm of values—aesthetic, moral, political values—the effects of teaching can only be indirect. Moral qualities are not the end result of a deliberate activity but arise out of practice, much as we develop a palate for good wine, an ear for music, or skill at a sport.

There are aspects of vocational practice that may result in fortunate educational experiences and are more likely to develop on the job: a taste for elegant solutions, the pleasure of a job well done, the esprit de corps that arises from an energetically pursued common task. Sam Florman, speaking of his own profession, has aptly spoken of "the existential pleasures of engineering."[1] Whatever the situational complications, it becomes immediately apparent that the "existential" dimensions of professional activity engage the *person* of the doer in a manner not provided for in the impersonal manner of how-to books and their equivalents in university instruction. As inspired leaders and gifted teachers know, where such joys are present, the task at hand will be better performed. But these pleasures are not in any instrumental sense the end of the activities that give rise to them. They have the sporting quality of enjoyment of the activity for itself. The better result of the task is a gift over and above the joy of performing it. Such transcending of the bounds of utility does not automatically put nobler goals in its place, as when what should be instrumental—like money—is pursued as a final end. Conquering Everest "because it's there" is noble in the most sporting way. Making yet another million, because there is yet another million to be made, is fetishism.

Well-meaning people, witnessing callous, unfeeling, unprincipled behavior, indifference to beauty, selfishness, and vulgarity often say: "Teach them values!" There is a natural desire for rules of conduct that are both simple and absolutely valid. One of the difficulties, however, is that values cannot be taught like multiplication tables or the laws of thermodynamics or the rules of grammar. They do not constitute a circumscribed body of knowledge to be acquired. They are not the matter of a subject to be added to and taken along with other subjects. Ethics and aesthetics have, of course, been taught as academic disciplines at least since Aristotle. But to teach and learn *about* values is not to impart or come to hold them. It is possible to teach politics in handbook form only when politics is stripped of all considerations of meaningful human existence in society and is viewed merely as the technique of power.[2] Values are not acquired as stock to be added to what one already happens to possess. They are not impersonal and cumulative aptitudes such as permit a division of labor. Professional ethics, for instance, does not mean that the doctor will do the medicine and the hospital ethicist will see to the morals; it means the doctor conducting his practice in an appropriate manner. Institutions, no doubt, require forensic experts, but ethical responsibility cannot be delegated. This is true of even the more peripheral, though not negligible, virtues. We can hire someone to teach us which fork to use and how to dance the quadrille, but politeness is something one has to internalize for oneself. To awaken and cultivate values is not to provide the learner with additional tools, not to add another facet to *what* he is—a neurologist, a scuba diver, a poor cook—but to bring about a change of *who* he is. Values are personal, or they are nothing.

Does this mean that values are simply subjective preferences and that it would be meaningless, perhaps even wrong, to try to affect them? If they cannot be taught discursively, can they be taught at all? Is there anything to be taught or is "values" just a fancy name we give our predilections? Should we simply adopt the disarming modesty of "I don't know very much about art, but I know what I like"? I don't think so. Such down-home candor conceals, in fact, an emphatic assertion of unexamined selfhood.

Educating aesthetic sensibility and ethical sensitivity is not an easy matter. Neither morality nor taste can be imposed. But they can, perhaps, be cultivated. Before we give up, we must consider, in any case, that if the ethical sense and the good taste of the young (and not so young) can be corrupted, it can, by the same token, be improved.

But how? The choice of appropriate means must be made in the light of desirable outcomes, about which there is little agreement. Many deplore the passing of a better age, when such things were supposedly clear. But the problem is hardly new. More than two thousand years ago, a judicious thinker wrote about the dilemmas of education:

> We have now to consider the nature of the education to be given. At present opinion is divided about the subject of education. All do not take the same view about what should be learned by the young, either with a view to plain goodness or with a view to the best life possible; nor is opinion clear whether education should be directed mainly to the understanding, or mainly to moral character. If we look at actual practice, the result is sadly confusing; it throws no light on the problem whether the proper studies to be followed are those which are useful in life, or those which make for goodness, or those which advance the bounds of knowledge. Each sort of study receives some votes in its favor; [none of them has a clear case]. If one looks, for example, at the studies which make for goodness, one finds a total absence of agreement. Goodness itself, to begin with, has not the same meaning for all the different people who honour it; and when that is the case, it is hardly surprising that there should also be a difference about the right methods of practicing goodness.[3]

No less a man than Milton thought that "the end of learning is to repair the ruin of our first parents."[4] Characteristically, like most educators who see education primarily as an instrumental enterprise, aiming at a purpose beyond itself, Milton wants to ground educational efforts not on the word, but on the knowledge of "sensible things . . . by orderly conning over the visible and inferior creature." "Language," he writes, "is but the instrument conveying to us things useful to be known." Even Milton, however, does not expect "the highest perfection" to be attained by learning unassisted by "heavenly grace and faith." The imperfection symbolized by the story of the Fall is part of the human condition and cannot be remedied by learning. That is why, as Mark Van Doren put it, nobody thinks he is educated.

> [It is] impossible to discover a man who believes that the right things were done to his mind. He was forced to learn too many things; or too few. It was all too general; or too special. The present was ignored; or the past. Something was left out entirely, or at best skimmed over: mathematics, poetry, the method of science, the secret of religion, the history of this or that . . . whereas once he did not care, now—if he is middle aged—he does. . . .

Perhaps no age has thought its education good enough. Life itself is never good enough and the job of education, which is to remedy the defect, doubtless cannot be done. If life were perfect, there would be no need of education. . . . But life remains imperfect, and so does education.[5]

The proper function of education is not really remedial at all. It is nurturing. Schools are neither hospitals nor houses of correction. They are not there to fix what is wrong, to heal what is ailing, to rehabilitate the straying mind. It is sad that institutions of so-called higher education are faced with the need to make up for the poor preparation of students in the lower schools; for example "remedial English," under a suitably euphemistic name, can now be taken for college credit. It is the price of social promotion with which educational achievement has failed to hold pace.

Still worse is the conception of education in the image of making, where the learner is thought of as matter to which something is done, to be stamped or melted and poured into a mold. The educator is neither a doctor nor a smith. He is much more like a gardener. The training he provides is more like the training of a growing vine than like the training of a recruit by a drill sergeant. Not all vines should be trained in the same fashion, and the same vine can be trained in different sensible ways. There are many different kinds of garden: more or less formal gardens, orchards, grand parks, and modest window boxes. One kind will be more suitable to a particular soil or climate than another. But given the many, indeed the endless possibilities—for there is, as we saw, little agreement about the "one best kind"—we can always tell the difference between a planned and tended garden and a patch of weeds or a slab of concrete. The artifice of education is there to guide the growth and help it flourish. A cultivated human being is just that. The only difference is that at some point—and in some measure, of course, from the beginning—a person becomes his own gardener.

Part 4

A Program

25

Courses of Study

What, then, should a cultivated human being be taught and how should he be taught? There will not be, it would seem, one best way.

One of the ways to pursue a liberal education is to follow a particular field of studies in a liberal spirit: history, physics, literature, philosophy, even economics, not in order to become a practitioner of that discipline—though that option need not be excluded—but in order to know what it means to know in the manner of an historian, as a physicist, etc., that is to say, to understand a particular mode of human inquiry and its terms of reference.

The learner acquires a sum of substantive knowledge, interesting in itself and, of course, essential to the process of learning, for no one can "learn how to learn" without actually learning some things. But beyond the skills and information conveyed by any particular discipline, the learner realizes that the terms of a proper inquiry are characteristic of a particular mode (historical, for example) of inquiry, and he can by extension, with due respect to those trained in other disciplines, imagine what it must mean to know in other modes that cut up reality in a different way. It will, above all, provide a partial but coherent introduction into the intellectual tradition in which the student stands and in reference to which he can discover, articulate and develop his aptitudes and the core of personality capable of integrating the various modes of experience that we call an identity.

A major and appropriate minors in suitable fields will be a more fruitful program of liberal education for those students whose family background and previous schooling have already provided a broad educational foundation, enabling them to make connections, recognize allusions, play with different modes of abstraction, use long words. Such students are also the ones most likely to suspend utilitarian considerations, making their undergraduate studies liberal in yet another sense.

Most professionals, regardless of schooling and upbringing, have the opportunity to pursue this kind of liberal education, focusing on a particular discipline, in their undergraduate years. Many, however, often under pressure from "sensible parents" who do not wish to see them wasting time in "childish" pursuits, prefer to emphasize pre-professional—for example, pre-med, pre-law—courses. Locke may be obsolete, according to Stanford's Associate Dean for Academic Programs, but readers of Plato will remember that parental philistinism is of all times: philosophy, is all very well for kids, thought Callicles, but mature men should be dealing with "serious" matters, such as money and power.[1] Engineers, on the other hand, are, generally speaking, denied the possibility of pursuing a more liberal education altogether, since their standard certification is the bachelor's degree.[2] It is evident that special arrangements are necessary to address their needs.

A person who has benefited from a thorough education in a discipline will know that there is no shortcut to understanding the principles and methods peculiar to any discrete mode of organizing human thought—certainly not that of his own specialty. But it is curious to observe how often people believe that, whereas their own field requires a careful and prolonged initiation, the essentials of other things—especially things they do not care for very much—can be picked up on the wing. As a result, they frequently propose "broadening the curriculum" and prescribe a sprinkling of this and that. Navy ROTC students, for example, pursuing engineering degrees in Boulder—and I imagine this is true with other services and at other universities—face a foreign language requirement of one (!) semester in order to be commissioned. The seriousness with which this requirement is regarded by the students and the quality of the educational outcome can be readily imagined.

Popularizing—making things intelligible to the nonspecialist—is a very difficult and intellectually demanding task. Oppenheimer, we saw, thought it quite impossible. It is in any case very different than providing a watered-down version of the "real thing," which is, sadly, though predictably, what survey courses for nonmajors generally tend to be. The people best suited to the task, those who possess the magisterial command of the subject that enables them to sum up and simplify with a minimum of distortion and a maximum of clarity, are least likely to be employed in an activity that offers few rewards and is far removed from the "cutting edge" of research, where professional reputations are made.

Most universities prefer instead to offer a very broad choice of courses and let the students select the offerings for which they feel the greatest aptitude, curiosity, or intellectual affinity. The system has the advantage of policing itself. The students are free to choose, and the teachers can cultivate in good conscience the areas of special interest to them. There is a degree of complicity in this, which may or may not work out to everyone's benefit. Though they may flatter themselves on their freedom of choice, students must in fact take the worth of any offered course of study on trust, for if they already knew all that it had to offer, they would hardly need to take it. They are, in the nature of things, immature and poorly informed and often moved by unexamined stereotypical expectations of both the nature of subjects offered and of their own aptitudes. For the teachers and educational planners, on the other hand, honoring the students' moral and intellectual autonomy can also serve as an excuse to avoid the responsibility of providing guidance. The manner in which students in their freedom choose the courses creates a further complicity. The better students naturally gravitate to the more demanding courses, whereas the weaker ones seek the less-taxing options. In this fashion they stream themselves with no need for authoritative intervention. The difficult but necessary task is to help give direction and yet allow for the full measure of freedom that is of a piece with the dignity of the students and that allows them, be it only for purely educational purposes, to make their own mistakes.

The untrammeled elective system is now frequently modified by the introduction of "core curricula." As the products of committees, which are inclined to seek widespread if weak support—or at least the absence of vociferous opposition—such "cores" are frequently very diluted and eclectic. The half-baked so-called core program at Harvard is a very good, though hardly rare, example of this. Core curricula raise questions of philosophical principle and ideological adherence and are therefore hotly contested. Their adoption can only be fruitful where the nature and circumstances of an institution make a meaningful consensus possible. Where agreement on cores can only be bought at the price of inanity, it is perhaps better to leave the elective system alone, and let it operate according to a logic that has much to recommend it, especially at large and rich institutions. Only two things are essential: to assure the scholarly integrity and quality of the offerings and to provide for a powerful network of academic advising. Counseling is perhaps the weakest aspect of university life and the one most in need of urgent and thoughtful care.

26

Humanist Education

There is another manner of imparting a liberal education, one which has undergone many transformations in its descent from humanism proper, that is, Renaissance humanism.[1] Rather than privilege a single voice in the learned conversation of mankind—history, science, literature—or seek to sample a variety of methods of inquiry in the form of electives, the student comes into contact with modes of thinking as expressed in primary manifestations, books and other works of a civilization. The classical world, as a variegated civilization, serves as a world of reference, both as a source of meaningful continuity and as a culture sufficiently distant to serve as a foil to immediate experience.

Humanist education is deliberately personal. The student is entrusted to a tutor, and the course of study is adapted to develop the potential of this particular student, suited to his unique idiosyncracy. It does not serve abstract educational goals except insofar as these are realized by making the best of the individual student.

The Renaissance man—and indeed woman[2]—is not a polymath, one who knows a lot of things, but one whose world of cultural reference allows him to place, evaluate, and appreciate the things he comes across. His education is not abstract science but a maturity of taste and judgment that becomes one with his personality. In this it is quite unlike scholastic education, which, in many ways against the precepts of its master, Aristotle, shears everyone over the same comb. And indeed, sociologically, the Renaissance gentleman, high civil servant, courtier, even scientist or artist stands in stark contrast to the lowly scholastically trained clerk, who may or may not rise in the ranks of the Church or one of its branches, such as the university.

Northern humanists like Erasmus sought to have it both ways, and before long the wisdom of the ancients was neatly packaged in textbooks for the use of schools, with the lessons to be drawn from the ancient texts conveniently premasticated. The search for teacher-proof methods of teaching has long antecedents.

Some balance between the need for a formal institutional framework and the personal nature of humane education was found in the English universities with their tutorial system. For a time, undergraduates would study practically the breadth of surviving texts of Greek and Roman antiquity from Homer to Pliny, from Thucydides to Horace, covering poetry, philosophy, natural science, and history—and that would be their university education.

In the long run, the advance of the natural sciences, not just in their utility and power, but as intellectual disciplines to be understood out of a liberal desire to know, could not be resisted. Neither could modern languages and literatures, whose force was further strengthened by awakened feelings of nationalism. Accordingly, modern subjects were introduced, that provided a different kind of initiation to the students' intellectual inheritance. All in all, as a complete undergraduate education, a comprehensive humanist scheme became difficult to uphold.

In the United States the idea of a humanist education based on the outstanding texts of the Western tradition has been effectively revived in very small colleges. The relatively rare predisposition of the students who choose to attend and the very close-knit community of tutors whose lives are centered on the college make it a model difficult to imitate on a larger scale. For most people—outside the special atmosphere of colleges where pedagogical structures and small size provide a rigor easily lost in a spread-out program of readings—thorough training in a specialized discipline is as much a crucial complement to a general education as the other way around. The broader appeal of text-centered liberal studies lies not so much in their capacity to provide a complete university education in themselves, as in their power to complement a vocational or otherwise specialized course of study. Moses Hadas, referring to the pioneering text-based general education program at Columbia University, writes,

> No teacher would be satisfied that his students were being properly educated if he did not know that they were concurrently subjected to the more rigorous disciplines of specialized education. Whereas the teacher of a specialized course proceeds on the assumption that his students are all embryo chemists or economists or philologers, the teacher of a General Education course knows that he is addressing amateurs and seeks to assist them to the widest and fullest possible understanding of their physical and social intellectual environment.[3]

27

The Civic Mission of the University

The personal and explanatory, rather than impersonal and prescriptive character of a liberal education is best served when one can create a community of learners who cooperate in an atmosphere where the necessary discipline is imposed as far as possible by the task itself rather than by a person in authority. These things, however, don't happen on their own; they too have to be learned. Putting a group of young people together and asking them to discuss a text can easily lead to superficiality and a lack of genuine exchange, in short, a time-wasting free-for-all. Guidance is needed.

A properly conducted seminar links the broadening of intellectual horizons to the student's personality, his intelligence to his integrity. It creates a community of speech and reason and then provides the conditions for what Barber calls the "civic mission of the University." The university, he writes, not only *has* a civic mission but, he continues, quite properly stressing the existential and personal dimension of education, it *is* a civic mission. "It is civility itself, defined as the rules and conventions that permit a community to facilitate conversation and the kind of discourse upon which all knowledge depends."[1]

The small discussion class is not the only possible manifestation of this spirit in the university, but it is certainly a privileged one. One need not go as far as Barber in identifying knowledge with "an evolving communal construction where legitimacy rests directly on the character of the social process" without any further validation from either tradition or independent reason, to agree with him in stressing that knowledge cannot be thought of separately from the workings of human sociability.

Hutchins argued that democracy requires a liberal education for all.[2] He maintained that uneducated political power is dangerous, and uneducated leisure is degrading. To the extent that in an affluent industrial democracy all exercise power and dispose of leisure, everyone, wrote Hutchins, requires a liberal education. What was traditionally considered the best education for the best, or the ruling few, becomes the best education for all. Barber wishes to "go beyond the old instrumental argument on behalf of democracy that rests the case for citizens training inside the university on the prudential need to shore up democracy outside the university."[3] Beyond Jefferson's formula of education as the guarantor of liberty, Barber advances the notion that "we not only have to educate every person to make him free, but we have to free every person to make him educable."[4]

The university as a free learning community promotes the art of civility creating, Barber writes, "a common language in the face of private differences." The university is in a strange situation with regard to society, a situation reminiscent of the father confessor kept in great noble houses of old. The good father must please the masters of the house to keep his bread and butter, but it is also his specific duty to scrutinize their motives and seek to check their appetites. The possibilities for corruption are evident and, on the whole, university corporations, who also know on which side their bread is buttered, have not been much more courageous than father confessors. But the principle is clear. Barber points out that neither the purist proponent of detached liberal education nor the advocate of vocational training recognizes how awkward it is

> for a liberal arts university at once to serve and challenge society, to simultaneously "transmit" fundamental values such as autonomy and free thinking and create a climate where students are not conditioned by what is transmitted. . . . For such a university must at once stand apart from society in order to give students room to breathe and grow free from a too insistent reality; and at the same time it must stand within the real world and its limiting conditions in order to prepare students to live real lives in a society that, if they do not mold it freely to their aspirations, will mold them to its conventions.[5]

There is, however, one illusion that we must guard against, and that is the historically given or logically necessary finality of democracy. Hutchins sees democracy as a final stage of a development, as the achievement—as yet imperfect perhaps—of the one perfectly just society. But there can be no such thing. Societies are held together by norms. That is what makes them societies. Norms—peculiar to a particular society, so that we have democratic norms in a democratic society—are binding in that those who conform to them, are rewarded, and those who do not are punished. Therefore, "there must always be at least that inequality of rank which results from the necessity of sanctioning behavior according to whether it does or does not conform to established norms."[6] Social norms are universal in the sense that they apply to everyone. The outcome of their operation, however, is not equality but stratification resulting from and expressing the relative conformity or deviance of social groups in relation to the dominant norms. But inequality causes discontent and leads to protest or rejection of the principles on which it is based, i.e., opposition to the norms characteristic of that particular society.

> Since human society without inequality is not realistically possible and the complete abolition of inequality is therefore ruled out, the intrinsic explosiveness of every system of social stratification confirms the general view that there cannot be an ideal, perfectly just and therefore non-historical human society.[7]

The freedom that Barber seeks for the university has the virtue of being both loyal and critical of society, its virtue not relative to the regime, but, as it were, at an angle to it.

Less certain, no doubt, about the degree to which democracy is actually realized, Barber goes a step further than Hutchins but in another direction. He makes truth itself "inasmuch as we can have it at all," depend on "conformity to communicative processes that are genuinely democratic and that occur only in free communities."[8] If, however, establishing the truth "inasmuch as we can have it at all" depends on realizing "genuinely democratic processes," how will we know, in truth, that we are getting closer? How, indeed, will we know what is truly anything—democratic, for instance—until we get there? If truth is merely a social construct, how will we, in fact, know that we are, or for that matter, that we are not there at all? As Wallace Stevens said, reality is only the basis, but it is the basis. Democracy will be sought and defended because people have good reason to want it, not because it wants itself.

28

Opportunities and Constraints

In the light of such considerations, how much can a program of humanities for engineers hope to accomplish? In designing such a program it is important to make the most of the advantages offered by general developments no less than by a particular setting.

Of general developments two are especially advantageous to the liberal education of engineers. The first is the change of attitude of potential employers. Industry, as we saw, has become increasingly aware of the need for versatile, articulate, broadly educated people whose nimble minds are able to cope with a rapidly changing technological and social environment. It has become clear to leaders in business and in government that a highly specialized technical competence will quickly become obsolete if it is not accompanied by a broader vision, a capacity to communicate well, and a willingness to keep up to date. If the motives of industry are primarily utilitarian, they represent very real human needs. Employers are understandably more interested in the side effects, as it were, of culture. But who wants the effect wants the cause.

The second general trend that is advantageous to liberal studies is a development within engineering education itself. Many schools have recognized the need to move toward a general grounding of their students in the engineering sciences that underlie the various professional specializations. The familiarity with science proper, with unifying principles of a higher degree of abstraction, is itself an element of general culture of the greatest importance, and it is formative of analytical habits of mind. Other subjects of overarching vocational interest, such as applied mathematics and engineering management, not only provide essential professional skills but also, where they exist independently, do not impinge, as they have on many occasions in the past, on the time and resources available for liberal studies. Students benefit, furthermore, from a general policy, consciously advanced by administrators and advisors, which invites students and instructors alike to pay greater attention to the organization and form of oral and written presentations in engineering courses themselves.[1]

Of the particular conditions favorable to a successful liberal studies program none has been stressed so much as administrative leadership. "At every institution where a lively program is under way we found that there had been one or more administrative officers—presidents, deans, department heads—who had worked hard in laying the groundwork."[2] The active support of key administrators affects the attitudes of faculty and staff. Such attitudes, in turn, naturally influence the outlook of students.[3]

Making the most of its opportunities and with a clear view of its goals, a program of humanities for engineers must be designed with an equally unclouded understanding of the institutional, cultural, and material constraints under which it must operate.

The most obvious constraint is time. In general, no more than six or seven required courses, or 12 to 18 credit hours, in the humanities and social sciences—including language and writing programs—find room in the standard four-year curriculum of about 130 required credit hours leading to the bachelor's degree in engineering. An extension of the curriculum leading to the established engineering certification in five or more years has been suggested by educators and has been adopted (often to be dropped again) by some schools. Given the eagerness of the students to qualify for professional employment in as short a period as possible and the competition between schools for enrollment, it is, in fact, unlikely that the longer curriculum will be broadly adopted in the near future. Even if it were adopted, it is not at all clear that it would lead to a significant increase in liberal studies. Past experience indicates that, given more time, not only are faculties more likely to increase the number of technical courses rather than allow for greater breadth and depth in general education, but the students themselves are inclined to structure the earlier part of their studies, supposedly dedicated to general studies, with an eye to the technical professional courses they anticipate taking in the years that follow. Students, in other words, given the opportunity for a preliminary "general" period of study are likely to transform it into a "pre-engineering" preparation. This may be desirable for other reasons, but it does little to enhance liberal studies.

Educators have thought of ensuring that engineers have a broad humane education in a different way: by means of entrance requirements. Nothing, of course, could be more desirable than to see the high school achieve its rightful place as the natural home of general education. It is conceivable that the need to prepare students for more exacting university entrance requirements would raise the sights of high schools and, combined with adequate material and moral support, would yield admirable results. Things being as they are, for now and the foreseeable future, universities will have to take students as they find them and strive to do their best by them.

The severe limitations of time impose certain choices on the design of a program of humanities for engineers. It is important not to proclaim grandiose aims while failing to make the best of limited opportunities. "As a whole, . . . statements of purpose indicate that many engineering educators consider the humanities and social sciences a kind of 'package' deal which will somehow miraculously fill in the gaps in the engineer's education."[4] Conversely, there is often an "alarming gap between the pretensions and the performance of the liberal arts."[5] The disparity between exaggerated expectations and real possibilities can only discredit programs of liberal studies for engineers.

The expansion of curricula in the hope of covering a growing number of subjects naturally leads to the dilution of the courses taught. It is evident that teaching programs must be rethought and restructured in order to keep pace with the development and differentiation of human knowledge. But it is not possible to expand existing teaching programs ad infinitum, in response now to this challenge, now to that. It is not just a matter of managing vast amounts of material. An educated human being must be informed, but an education, I have argued, is not a heap of information. Critical habits of mind and a maturity of judgment do not, of course, develop in the abstract. Skills are always linked to factual knowledge, to stuff, but they are not the stuff. "In all humanistic-social work the objective must be not 'coverage of subject matter' but development of interest and enthusiasm *together* with sufficient knowledge that the student may continue his reading at his leisure and with some confidence that he knows what he is doing."[6]

There is another set of difficulties in designing a humanities course for engineers. The difficulties arise from the different perception of the task at hand by engineering and humanities faculty, and poor communication between them.

Engineering faculty, normally charged with the responsibility of advising their students in the selection of their courses, are likely to know little and too frequently care less about liberal studies in general and the humanities classes taught at their institution in particular.[7] In practice, too many students are simply told to enroll in anything that will satisfy the Accreditation Board for Engineering and Technology (ABET) and College requirements. Conversely, Arts and Science faculty and, sadly, many university administrators tend to think that the introductory courses designed for liberal arts majors are perfectly adequate for the purposes of engineering students as well. They see no reason for special programs at all, beyond some form of coordination of existing course offerings.[8]

Some courses, no doubt, prove to have universal appeal. Departmental specialization, however, means that introductory courses are intended to prepare students for later courses in the same subject. Such courses often have a technical preparatory character, emphasizing the mastery of materials and techniques essential for more advanced work in the particular discipline in question. They are not designed as general education courses for the nonspecialist, which are the sort of courses engineering students need.[9] Engineers need to approach liberal studies in a liberal spirit, not in the manner of someone seeking to make a humanities subject his field of professional competence. This is not a call for the lowering of academic standards for the benefit or, rather, to the detriment of engineering students. Engineering students are among the most able on any campus. Measured by SAT scores, high school class standing, and other measures of aptitude, they are often the best. On the contrary, what is needed are demanding programs taking advantage of the generally excellent working habits of engineering students, programs that can maintain their interest in a manner that preparatory classes cannot. The goal of such programs must be, however, to produce educated laymen, not trained technicians in a discipline, no matter how "liberal" the discipline itself may be thought to be. That a general education requires a familiarity with methods of investigation in the disciplines it embraces, not just with a survey of results, goes without saying, but the skills required, outside one's own discipline, are those of the knowledgeable critic, not of the master craftsman.

There are other disadvantages to liberal studies being made available to engineering students mainly in the form of preexisting departmental introductory courses. Engineering students often feel intimidated in a setting that puts them at a disadvantage with respect to verbally more agile, though not necessarily more gifted, fellow students who "belong" in the departmental courses that the engineering students are visiting.

The virtual divorce of research from undergraduate teaching means, furthermore, that most classes available to engineering students, and supposedly suitable for them, are taught by instructors whose heart is in the graduate work and the writing on which their careers depend. It is, ironically, the strong departments, the ones one would in principle wish to draw on, that are most likely to have this flaw.

Most departments, as soon as they grow strong enough, begin to think seriously about the advantage of having graduate students as apprentice scholars in the disciplinary enterprise and as teaching assistants. . . . As senior staff members increasingly devote their attention to research and advanced teaching, and as more courses become the province of teaching assistants, the quality of education available to masses of general students often suffers.[10]

All undergraduate teaching at institutions with graduate programs suffers from the greater scholarly and professional rewards held out by research and publishing. But of all undergraduates, those who suffer the most are those who have the least time to lose. The damage for the general student is compounded by the natural tendency of scholars, precisely to the degree that they are primarily professional scholars rather than teachers, to specialize and to be more interested in their chosen subjects of study than in the general education of students.

One might suppose that the humanist and social scientist each would perceive at once his primary mission as the development of a critical attitude among engineering students.

Unfortunately, the humanist, at least according to the campus reports, seems little disposed to accept this assignment. His professional attention is focused on a subject matter, and his professional view is a fragmented one: he is an 18th century man; his field is the novel; he is a specialist in classical drama. And while any of these areas may involve a great deal which has to do with human values and the human condition, such matters are seldom his first concern. Graduate school has trained him to concentrate on certain pieces of the overall field, and he has been indoctrinated with the idea that the road to success is through further specialization, scholarly publication, and the training of graduate students who will perpetuate this process.[11]

A program of instruction is only as good as the people who teach it. It is important that the program be directed and implemented in the main by people who owe their primary allegiance to the program and who do not feel displaced in a school of engineering. "The best instruction comes . . . from a staff that understands and likes engineering students. Very little is accomplished by an instructor who wishes he were doing something else, or who regards himself as a martyred missionary among technically-minded Philistines."[12] Such staff, trained in the humanities, pure science and the social sciences, but loyal to their engineering students, are the best mediators between the needs of the students and the offerings in Arts and Science. Given the established pattern of rewards, material and moral, which in present-day universities favors departmental specialization, research, and publication, that is not always easy. In fact, the single greatest difficulty in keeping general humanities programs afloat is recruiting and holding on to gifted and dedicated teachers. Every effort must be made, therefore, to provide compensation that can make up for possible disadvantages to the staff in terms of professional advancement normally linked to departmental career structures.

A successful program of humanities for engineers must rest on instructors who like to teach and who, though well versed in the humanities, do not feel "wasted" on engineers. There are among the faculty in Arts and Science people who see bringing humanities to engineers as a stimulating challenge and who would welcome the opportunity to advance general education in a liberal spirit.

Professional advancement in the university is normally linked to departmental career patterns. A service department in a school of engineering, devoted to *teaching* humanities must make special provisions in order to attract and keep the good teachers it needs. No single pattern will suit every institution. In some the opportunity of combining technical and historical or theoretical interests will prove attractive to a gifted faculty.[13] In others the teaching itself, the opportunity of leading small classes, the challenge of awakening the dormant side of young people who have opted in principle for professional training, will be seen as a welcome opportunity for professional growth. In others again, what will be most attractive will be the freedom from the strictures of departmental limitations and the chance to do more than pay lip service to interdisciplinarity. In all cases, however, forms of recognition and compensation must be found to make up for the sacrifice of the orthodox path of advancement. Where that is not the case, a program of humanities for engineers will end up with hand-me-downs from English or other humanities and social science departments, whom neither their colleagues nor their students will esteem, and who will themselves feel cheated and martyred by a capricious fortune.

29

The Text-Based Seminar

Thoughtful commentators have pointed out that, in order to satisfy the need for a liberal education of special students, such as engineering students, whose focus of academic endeavor lies outside the humanities and social sciences, "neither a discipline-oriented approach, with its emphasis in a specific subject matter, nor the kind of interdisciplinary approach which attempts to 'cover' impossible chunks of material is satisfactory."[1] A recent report, based on a broad and thorough survey, recommended "clustering" electives in liberal studies.[2] A carefully designed program of text-based discussion classes goes, I believe, beyond clusters in the same direction, allowing students to become familiar with different, nontechnical patterns of meaningful inquiry, seen as modes of the pursuit of knowledge in its fundamental unity. In text-based classes, the students come into contact with a variety of utterances of human self-understanding, poetic, historical, philosophical, scientific, not in the form of excerpts of textbook knowledge, arranged by disciplines separated from one another for the convenience of academic research, but as original achievements of the human mind, as masterpieces in their formal integrity.

All pertinent studies seem to be unanimous in extolling the pedagogic advantages of small discussion groups. The small seminar brings about a community of learning. Physical arrangements are not unimportant in achieving this end. It is always advisable for all participants to sit around a table facing each other rather than have students sit in rows facing a teacher. Where possible, the presence of two moderators further diminishes the usual schoolroom polarity between teacher and pupils.

The purpose of the seminars is to *discuss* the readings and the questions arising from them, not to *present* the materials. The task of the moderators is not so much to instruct, as to guide the discussion. Participants enter and drop out of the conversation without raising of hands, as they would in a lively, but polite social occasion. The rules are those of common courtesy and those of intellectual responsibility and honesty: letting others have their say; not merely asserting one's own opinion but giving reasons for it; respecting the person of each of one's interlocutors while—possibly—disagreeing with his ideas. The aim is not to display one's learning or to score points but to learn to entertain an argument and to examine the structure of a train of thought—including one's own. The success of the seminars depends on the active participation of all members.

In discussing the meaning of a poem, the structure of an argument or the validity of a demonstration, students learn to examine their own convictions, to listen attentively to the opinions of others, to engage in a conversation that leads away from holding and stating unreflected "points of view" to a responsible consideration of ideas. In this manner they develop habits of intellectual rigor paired with civility and conversational ease.

The process is not easy, and it is far from automatic. The deep-seated habit of viewing the teacher as purveyor and the pupil as consumer of information, which the pupil can then reproduce to the teacher's satisfaction, is hard to break. The usual classroom attitude is, if anything, reinforced by the great amount of factual learning that goes on in an engineering school. A great deal of goodwill and moral courage is required on the part of the students, skill and self-control on the part of the moderators. The moderators must resist the temptation to lecture, to hasten to give the "right" authoritative answer, to fill the uncomfortable silence, that may well be a pause for reflection leading to further insights. A highly directive, discursively didactic seminar, confirms the student's stereotypical expectation of the respective roles of teacher and learner, enhances the student's passivity and inhibits the opening of the learner's mind which is the principal aim of the small discussion group. And yet the moderators must guide, move a languishing conversation along, prevent a conversation from straying into abject generality or trivial detail, encourage the students to converse, to look at each other, speak to each other and listen to each other.

Ideas cannot be taught outright; insight cannot be induced. But what one can and ought to do is create conditions favorable to the reception of ideas and to real understanding. Each human mind must make its own discoveries. And yet the moderator must recognize the limit where it is perhaps better that the students be told something than that they discover nothing. Though he must, certainly, refrain from putting words in the students' mouths, in the metaphorical sense, the moderator must at the same time help the students develop a vocabulary by means of which to articulate and by so doing think through and deepen their responses, not only to the text before them but to a richer texture of reflected experience. The texts themselves are, of course, powerful teachers illuminating each other, but they are not enough in any normally possible university course to overcome the conceptual poverty characteristic of most contemporary high school graduates, without the benefit of thoughtful mediation.

The temptation to make sure you "get the right answer," at the expense of preventing it from being the *students'* answer, is matched by an equivalent and opposite temptation to consider good teaching primarily a matter of removing impediments to artless spontaneous learning. At its worst, the latter attitude invites sloth on the part of the teacher and encourages a lack of rigor of thought and expression on the part of the students. The moderator must then be self-effacing and eminently present at the same time, which is a difficult balance to maintain. But that too can be learned, not so much by precept as—ideally—by conducting such seminars in the company of a conscientious and competent partner. The proper balance will, in any case, not always be the same but will vary according to the nature of people and circumstances. No two seminars are alike and there is no teacher-proof method of teaching.

But what about content? What manner of texts should be the object of seminar discussions? Studies show that engineering students profit most from literature courses that emphasize ideas and values, as opposed to those that emphasize formal analysis or historical significance. "It did not seem to make much difference whether the literature was American, British, or Greek, so long as it dealt with important ideas and was aesthetically valuable in its own right."[3] What is true of literature is true of other forms of expression. Texts should be chosen then, because they are outstanding utterances of man's understanding of himself and of his world, formally admirable compositions that affect the terms in which we think, touch our deepest emotions, feed our intellectual appetite, arouse our aesthetic sensibility and speak to ever-recurring questions of human existence.

To transform the student's manner of learning, to lead to the discovery of what lies behind textbook knowledge as its fountain and origin, to liberate the student from the ready-made formulas of current opinion, the texts must be classics, i.e., fine examples of their kind.

Are there such works? Some works, it is true, enjoy an undeserved vogue, others remain undeservedly obscure. Allowing for the vicissitudes of intellectual fashion, literary quality, depth of feeling, elevation of thought, perspicacious observation, wit and methodical clarity are not, as some contemporary voices would have us believe, illusions created by astute and interested promoters now of this, now of that persuasion. Some books have charmed, seduced, compelled readers to take them up again and again, often generation after generation.

With this in mind, texts can be carefully selected, and these can, in principle and practice, be replaced by other texts. No one is compelled to choose between accepting and rejecting a breviary and its lessons. As we saw, it does not much matter exactly which texts the students study, as long as these works raise fundamental questions and each is aesthetically valuable in its own right.[4] Readings can be replaced by other readings, but not by *any* other readings.

The student who seeks to possess such well-wrought texts as mere things finds that they elude his immediate grasp. The meaning of the texts is never given in a manner that can be exhaustively wrapped up in a summary. The encounter is, then, more a challenge than a conquest. Unable to take what is there and run away, the student is induced to follow an invitation to pursue the intellectual adventures intimated by the text. This shift in attitude, in the manner of learning, is encouraged by the seminar discussion. The variety of sensibilities, aptitudes and outlooks of the several students, being brought to bear on a rich text, reveal many possible interpretations that do not necessarily exclude each other. Conversely, texts that can support different interpretations help develop the provisory suspension of judgment essential to fruitful discussion and the respect for the other human being, one's fellow in the seminar.

It has often been suggested by educationists and others that current events and burning issues of the day would be an appropriate focus for group discussions. It is thought that such topics would engage the interest of the students and at the same time prepare them for an active life of participatory citizenship. Yet, despite their intrinsic importance and the fact that students should be deeply concerned about such matters, controversial issues of this kind prove to be ill suited for seminar discussions.[5] The passionate engagements that they bring into play induce the participants to defend their convictions rather than discuss their ideas. Not only vociferous invective but also defiant silence is damaging to the fabric of a community of learning. Either way, the mechanisms of an assertive attachment to one's point of view, because it is one's own, runs counter to the fragile process of cooperative learning. Students naturally bring to the seminar their beliefs and opinions received from the world of their everyday experience. The seminar, however, is meant to help them reach inside themselves and *examine* their convictions and, at the same time, to reach outside themselves in the effort to understand their fellows. Learning to detach oneself from one's fervently held opinions, so closely linked to one's sense of identity and purpose, is a difficult process that requires a great deal of intellectual courage. It is important to create conditions favorable to the task of self-examination, and they require both a suspension of immediate utilitarian considerations and a measure of detachment from the passionate engagements of the day.

We cannot learn from what is too familiar because we are too close to it to see it in perspective. The justified expectation that education should be relevant is defeated by the easy and, at first sight, convincing response of taking what is current to be relevant. Courses proliferate in the vain attempt to catch up with the latest trend, to respond to the most recent crisis, to take advantage of the next opportunity in sight, and they become obsolete almost before they have been properly set up, for it is the nature of the current to run its course. Only yesterday we were urged, for instance, to concentrate, in the name of perceived relevance, on the "Pacific Rim" (by which no one seems to refer to the Aleuts or the Maori), before we were overtaken by events in Eastern Europe, that few people would have so much as imagined but a very short time ago, events which open quite unexpected vistas of hope and danger, of opportunity and responsibility.

It would be wrong to train the students of today to deal with the unpredictable problems and challenges of tomorrow in terms of what is relevant today, even if what is truly relevant could be clearly established. That, however, is itself far from certain. Some problems, it is clear, are pressing and should be studied. But relevance itself is not self-evident: it cannot be determined upstream from thinking.

On such grounds it may seem advisable to include works drawn from outside the Western tradition, not in the vain hope of creating the equivalent of a museum of exoskeletal types, but in order to satisfy and stimulate the natural curiosity of students, inviting them to the play of engagement and detachment with manifestations of human creativity. That some students may feel attracted to a seminar program by external signs of continuity or identification pertinent to themselves which certain texts seem to hold out to them, or by a taste for the evidently unfamiliar can be a welcome side effect. It must be said, however, that students, on the whole, are very far from having even a rudimentary idea of the contours of what might be called the Western tradition, and that the eagerness to "expand" their consciousness beyond "Eurocentric" parameters appears ludicrous if "Eurocentric" means anything like a reflected awareness of a complex historical heritage.

Indeed, one of the greatest impediments to a proper education is the assumption on the part of many students and, sadly, by an increasing number of their teachers, that they already know all they need to know about "the West," because of unreflected attitudes they acquired growing up in America or, indeed, just because they are white. Nothing, alas, could be further from the truth. A particular mode of anti-intellectual parochialism takes the form of more or less conscious synecdoches, i.e., of taking the part for the whole: secularized puritanism stands for "white America"; "white America" for "Europe," as the term is used in, for example, "Eurocentric"; "Europe" stands, in turn, for the "Western tradition," to include, presumably, the *Book of Job,* but to exclude, of all things, "Hispanidad." The presumption that "white America" somehow subsumes the European experience strikes the European as poorly informed and narrowly self-referential.

It is, nonetheless, a matter of even greater delicacy to introduce students to symbolic forms and worlds of complex cultural reference to which they bring no more than candid curiosity. Some misreadings, such as the effect of Far Eastern paintings or of African Art on European aesthetic sensibility, have been fruitful in their own way. Hasty "assimilation" is, however, more an impediment than a vehicle of understanding the creative acts that it seeks to absorb on their own terms. The "broadening of horizons" must, therefore, be done responsibly, patiently, modestly, or not be done at all. It involves as much conscious examination of what one already has and is, as further acquisitions, leading to the novelty of what one learns to become. We do not overcome our parochialism by opening boxes of different shape and color and reading the instructions.

Seminar readings can be arranged in several meaningful ways, and one can always make a good case for chronological order. One can, however, arrange them instead according to didactic principles in order to help the students adapt to the requirements of a participatory discussion class.[6]

One can ensure, for instance, that earlier readings tell a story and are, as such, easy to follow and to enjoy. The relative simplicity of narrative form makes it easier for all participants to engage the text. Responses will differ, of course, depending on what each seminar member brings to the reading. However, it is more likely that students will be inclined to suspend unexamined predilections and distastes when discussing a more or less straightforward account of a course of events. Gradually, and with proper guidance, students learn to distinguish which ideas are well supported by the text and which are not. Respect for the text, then, becomes a touchstone for mutual respect in the group.[7] The group comes together as a community of learning even as each of its members develops his capacity of critical, that is also self-critical, discussion.

The narrative text underlying the discussion need not be an actual literary text but may instead be a "readable" work of art. Given the limitations of reproduction this is most likely to be a painting and should at this stage be representational. This transfer to a nonliterary medium of the same notion of fidelity, attention to structure, composition, and other traditional elements of written communication, is not only a valuable exercise in itself, opening new dimensions of aesthetic sensibility, but also clarifies what is required when facing a text. The discovery that *seeing* a painting involves a great deal more than a nervous tingle or a pleasant or indifferent sensation that seems beyond further elucidation is a great and joyous step for most students. There is also a very noticeable shift in the way the seminar group comes together as each student looks up from the text or small reproduction before him to the one common object projected on the large screen before everyone. The students then turn to each other in a completely new way. The visibly common object of reference helps liberate the students from the self-referential closure of what they take to be incommunicable and therefore also unassailable private readings of "their" text and helps open them to the idea of giving a reasoned account of their responses.

The narrative texts can be arranged so that stories told in the third person, "from the outside," are succeeded by autobiographical pieces in which authors reveal themselves not only by means of the story they tell but also by the manner in which they tell it. As the importance of artistry in writing becomes increasingly apparent, it makes sense, then, to choose short, complete pieces, written in English—that is, not translations—before moving on to works of greater complexity.

The group can then move to the next stage. Dramatic texts heighten the student's sense of a meaningful structure, which is significant without being direct. The distinction between the narrator and his story, already intimated in the first part of the course can now become a clearer understanding of characters distinct from an author who has placed them in a context within which alone they make sense. Analytic texts, in turn, require close attention to logical development, to the structure of an argument.

It is not without some difficulty that students accept that the truth of a proposition can be discussed in terms other than those of subjective conviction—except of course in "science," i.e., natural science, whose propositions they are altogether *too* ready to accept as objectively compelling. This is one reason for including among the texts studied a class of readings which may be thought superfluous for students in a college of applied science: classics of science. In fact, students generally encounter science at the level of results presented in textbook form as a preparation for practical applications. The seminar gives them the opportunity to see science at the level of investigation, as the methodical unfolding of a thinker's intelligence, conversing with contemporaries and with predecessors. Science emerges as a distinctive mode of reasoning within an intellectual universe, in which the scientist shares as man of letters, as statesman, as explorer, as human being.

Having cleared the ground, the class can finally turn to introspective or self-examining texts. Narrative structures, dramatic context, well-framed arguments, which the student has learned to respect and to follow, now reveal a personal focus of experience which, in turn, affects the person, not merely the mind of the reader. This core of experience, which compels the reader to face himself, is not seen, however, in the light of unexamined sentiment; it is conveyed instead by intellectual rigor and a disciplined command of form.

Naturally, few texts belong, in themselves, in any one category, and some can be read now in one manner, now in another. Also, in practice some variation will be introduced, especially in the later parts of the sequence, to allow for a change of pace.

Supported by an atmosphere of civility and mutual responsibility, students acquire habits of attention, exactitude and discrimination, and develop criteria of validity appropriate to different modes of thought. They acquire intellectual virtues and a taste for excellence that will continue with them throughout their lives. By extension they develop standards of conduct, derived not so much from precepts they find in their readings—for such injunctions are always incomplete and bound to particular circumstances so that one set of precepts contradicts another—but from the manner in which they learn to discuss the texts.

The manifold human situations made present by the texts is not experienced as a series of raw, opaque happenings, but as a world of meaningful events, whose meaning is not so much fixed as illuminated by the art of the works under study. Finding their bearings in this world induces readers to become not only intellectually but also morally articulate.

Men, as we said earlier, do not become good by being told to be good. No course about ethics can make a bad man better. No course about values can create values, which can only spring from the moral freedom of man. But one can cultivate a moral disposition and help what are inchoate sentiments grow into a maturity of judgment. What the students bring with them, the familiar world of immediate and, therefore, also unreflected experience, becomes more lucid in the play of recognition and nonrecognition induced by the readings. The mirroring of their world in the partially recognized world of the texts allows them to discern the outline of their own makeup. This awareness, in turn, permits a clearer understanding of the text. It is in this oscillation that each student's world becomes more coherent, more of a world.

Seminars also provide excellent opportunities for writing. Unlike many conventional writing courses, a seminar will not be at a loss for themes "to give the student something to write about." The rich texts and lively discussions provide both stimulus and discipline. The writing gives the student an opportunity to go over the discussion and reflect on the effect it had on his original reading. Trying to fix his thought in writing, he is stimulated to reconsider and think further. The references to the text and to the discussion make it possible, at the same time, to limit rambling associations and to focus the presentation.

Last, not least, small discussion classes have an informal but nonetheless important function. On large, impersonal campuses they provide a special haven, giving rise to spontaneous exchanges that can be every bit as valuable educationally and personally as the conversations in the formal setting of the seminars. The taste for probing and wide-ranging discussion and the habits of conversational civility spill over into the students' everyday life. This is especially valuable given the heavy load and highly structured pattern of study of engineering students, which sets narrow limits to extracurricular activities, such as museum visits and film clubs, that would otherwise have been of great value in rounding off their liberal education.

In an ideal world, a formal education would have three stages, which, though they would naturally flow into each other, could be distinguished in principle. In elementary schooling fundamental tools would be acquired, such as a secure command of grammar, speed at doing sums, the ability to read with exactitude and ease—all the basic skills without which the world is a closed book and the lack of which makes for a lifelong inadequacy and wasteful and shameful attempts to cover up. If drill is necessary, then drill there must be; if "progressive" methods work, so much the better. In a secondary education, where aptitudes cannot be recognized in advance, before they have had a chance to manifest themselves in response to the opening of hitherto barely known or even quite unsuspected horizons, a considerable body of information in several areas should be provided and taken by the student on trust. The meaning of a poem will be revealed in a much fuller sense as life and further reading bring new depth to what was at first perhaps just a pleasing jingle. An understanding of the workings of the scientific imagination will eventually illuminate the Second Law of Thermodynamics, learnt at first just because teacher said one had to. Even vanity and snobbery have their place in what I call here secondary education: they are traps of the mind. You "approach" a great work with "admiration" because you think—you were told—you *ought* to admire it, and it actually reaches out and grabs you and leads you to places you didn't know existed, making your teacher's conventional admiration of it seem laughable in retrospect, or making you recognize that maybe there was more to what the old fool was saying than you thought at first. Only then, properly equipped and no doubt also made a little uncertain by a secondary education (and it is never a precise succession in time), is one capable of a liberal and, beyond it, of an enlightened professional education.

As it is, the university must do it all, and the methods will be mixed. Some of the work that needs to be done is remedial, some authoritative and informative, and some invites the delicate suspension of judgment, the sifting of evidence, the apprenticeship to real thinking that is true university work.

In his admirable book *The Civilized Engineer,* Sam Florman defends the dignity of engineering even as he seeks to encourage its practitioners to be rounded, humane human beings as well. He calls upon the poets of classical antiquity in defense of his notion of a humanity embracing both the artistic and the technical sphere against what he takes to be the anti-technical prejudice of the philosophers. He contrasts the esteem for technology found in Sophocles, for example, to the snobbish contempt for its practitioners that he attributes to "Plato and his cronies."[1] He is, I think, too quick to take offense. I take issue with this point in Florman's book because I think it weakens the drift of his otherwise excellent argument. His own examples of model "civilized engineers," like the Roeblings who designed the Brooklyn Bridge, were precisely not "living refutations of Plato's stereotype." They were, as Florman shows, people with a broad education and a grasp of theoretical understanding far beyond the vocational training advocated in the Morill Act. Plato would be in complete agreement with Florman that such training is poor preparation for freedom and citizenship. But Florman's irritation raises important questions. Certainly, in a society in which the division of labor was not very far advanced, crafty Ulysses built his own marriage bed, and circumspect Penelope did some (the ritually important part) of her own weaving.[2] But neither derived his rank or dignity from the productive work of his hands, whereas Andromache had every reason to fear the bitter necessity that would drive her, after the fall of Troy, to slave away at other peoples' looms.[3] In most societies, to work with one's hands or even to have to work for a living at all, rather than fight and hunt or enjoy some other kind of leisurely existence, rarely brought with it honor and prestige. Furthermore, the onus is hardly limited to technical occupations in Florman's sense, and many a man of letters—who is to the scribe as the engineer is to the technician—has had to swallow his pride before an illiterate nobleman or chieftain, or an uncouth industrialist for that matter. The affirmation of ordinary life, and, in particular, the recognition of the worth of the everyday life of production, was a long time coming.[4]

It is only in recent centuries that there has been a reversal of value.

Work, any work, seems to legitimate itself, and it is leisure and reflection that need to be justified. Leisure is legitimate as "rest and recreation," i.e., insofar as it is subordinate to work, as a means to an end.[5] Where this is not visibly the case, leisure is easily scorned as sloth. Such a reversal undoubtedly liberates creative capabilities and tends to relieve human beings from ascriptive bonds—including snobbery, perhaps—but it also channels all human activity into the same grand but aimless stream.

It is no doubt true, as Florman says, that snobbish values prevented gifted people from embarking on engineering careers. It is also true that many of these people rationalized their attitude by appealing to what they took to be the values of classical antiquity. But the problem raised by the ancient philosophers cannot be disposed of by pointing to their alleged snobbery. That problem has two sides: the first is that mindless toil, far from building character, demeans men and that citizenship and the meaningful exercise of freedom require a modicum of leisure. One needn't go to ancient history to draw this lesson. The autobiography of Frederick Douglass gives a poignant account of what the condition of slavery does to the slave's mind and soul and therefore to his very capacity for freedom.[6] It is, of course, largely thanks to modern technology, which makes the "shuttles in a loom fly to and fro by themselves,"[7] that it is possible not to restrict political activity and the possibility of the good life to those who have leisure, but to seek instead to extend the necessary leisure to all, who, in virtue of their humanity, are entitled to the pursuit of happiness. It is not by social convention, but by force of nature that necessity compels, and a life commanded by necessity is unfree.[8]

There are, no doubt, essential human satisfactions to be found in work itself and beyond these, as another of Florman's apt titles puts it, *The Existential Pleasures of Engineering*.[9] But if one doesn't work like one takes to drink, i.e., in order to keep one's mind off the things one does not want to face, the purpose and manner of the work is decisive. Cut off from meaning, as leisure is reduced to sloth, work becomes inhuman. This brings us to the second side of the ancient philosophers' argument. There are two kinds of activities: those that are an end in themselves, like contemplation, or sports or the good life as a whole— activities that are therefore liberal—and those that serve purposes beyond themselves, that are instrumental to other purposes, subordinate therefore to those other purposes, and in that sense servile. Professional sports, for example—strictly speaking, a contradiction in terms—are servile exactly to the extent that they are engaged in with a view to material gain. Now, technology is essentially instrumental and, though potentially satisfying as an intellectual exercise and as the means of tangible realizations of human projects, it cannot possibly determine its own ends. It may be, as Florman writes, "that the glory of Athens rested upon the marvels of Greek technology"—a statement not beyond discussion in the comparative study of civilizations—but the conditions of possibility are not the reasons for which anything is done. A skyscraper rests on foundations, but it is not snobbery to say that the penthouse is more desirable than the basement. What the penthouse comes to *stand for,* because it is desirable, is a separate matter. The Parthenon is, in a sense, a technical feat, but it is even more an embodiment of proportion and aesthetic balance; a "useless" building, furthermore, serving no productive purpose whatsoever, but rather the expression of the Athenians' sense of religious and civic meaning.[10] Thinking *is* better than doing, though Florman resents Plato for saying so,[11] because thought guides, or ought to guide, the deed.

It is wrong, perhaps, to separate thinking and doing, words and deeds. What the chorus of the *Antigone* sings, is not, as Florman writes, a "hymn to technology," but a powerful, indeed tragic reflection on human resourcefulness.[12] Florman quotes R. C. Jebb's translation:

> Wonders are many, and none is more wonderful than man; the power that crosses the white sea, driven by the stormy south-wind, making a path under surges that threaten to engulf him; . . . turning the soil with the offspring of horses, as the ploughs go to and fro from year to year. . . . And speech and windswift thought, and all the moods that mould a state, hath he taught himself; and how to flee the arrows of the frost, when 'tis hard lodging under the clear sky, and the arrows of the rushing rain; yea, he hath resource for all.[13]

Besides ships and plows and shelter against the elements, the Theban women sing of speech and thought and statecraft. Just as sailing the stormy seas is precarious, so also in all the other fields of intelligent and diligent human activity man's cleverness can lead to either "good or ill."[14] The "wonder" that is man according to the first line of the choral song, is a terrible wonder, not merely admirable, but awesome, dreadful *deinon.* Human ingenuity, the exercise of man's creative freedom, is intrinsically ambiguous.

A perfect being, like the God of Genesis, has no difficulty in reconciling words and deeds: "Let there be light: and there was light."[15] In divine omniscience and omnipotence there is no distinction between Word and Deed—and the Hebrew word *Dabar* tellingly translates as either.[16]

For man, however, bringing together words and deeds is no easy task. There are empty words, confusing and misleading words as well as meaningful, clarifying and revealing words. Deeds, on the other hand, can be opposed to mere words, as reality is opposed to illusion, but also as brute fact is opposed to articulate thought or as dumb force is opposed to speech and understanding.

The ambiguities of speech are bewildering, the simplicity of force captivating. Unable to admit a first principle as elusive and apparently weak as the Word, Faust struggles with the translation of St. John's Gospel:

> It is written: "In the beginning was the *Word!*"
> I'm stopped already. Who will help me further?
> I cannot possibly rate the *Word* so highly.
> I must translate it otherwise,
> if I am rightly enlightened by the spirit.
> It is written: "In the beginning was the *Thought!*"
> Consider the first line well,
> lest the pen write too hastily.
> Is it the *Thought* that works and creates all?
> Should it not be: "In the beginning was the *Power?*"
> Yet even as I write it down
> I feel I can not let it stand
> The spirit helps me! Suddenly I have it,
> and confidently write: "In the beginning was the *Deed!*"[17]

The poodle, which will prove to be Mephistopheles, is already in the study. Faust's departure from the Word leads in the course of events to unspeakable deeds. Pried away from the word, the deed is dreadful.

Man cannot rest in his works. God himself, Thomas Aquinas tells us, "who made all things, did not rest *in* those things . . . but rested *in* himself *from* the created works."[18] Be that as it may, man, an imperfect, timebound being, doesn't have that kind of self and cannot—short of grace, perhaps—fully reconcile the ambiguities of his creative freedom. To entertain this ambiguity without yielding to the delusory certitudes of practice and its promise of power is the mark of a civilized human being, not least of a civilized engineer. Man will work and do, but it is giving voice to his intimations of meaning, trusting the evidence of things not seen, that will justify his works. In the beginning was the word.

Notes

Introduction

1. Jean-Jacques Rousseau, *The Social Contract,* trans. Maurice Cranston, 48.

2. See the excellent historical summary in Edwin J. Holstein, Earl D. McGrath, *Liberal Education and Engineering,* 20ff. William Elgin Wickenden, *Report of the Investigation of Engineering Education, 1923–1929;* H. P. Hammond, "Engineering Education After the War," *Toward an Engineering Education,* vol. 24, no. 9 (May 1944): 589–613.

The goals and recommendations put forward by the Hammond report are restated in Edwin S. Burdell, *General Education in Engineering: A Report of the Humanistic-Social Research Project,* and again in E. A. Walker, J. M. Pettit, G. A. Hawkins, *Goals of Engineering Education, Final Report,* app. 2, 63. Specifically related to our theme is Sterling P. Olmstead et al., *Liberal Learning for the Engineer.*

For recent analyses see Joseph S. Johnston, Jr., Susan Shaman, Robert Zemsky, *Unfinished Design: The Humanities and Social Sciences in Undergraduate Engineering Education,* with its offshoot, an attractive guide for students and their advisors, *An Engineering Student's Guide to the Humanities and Social Sciences.* Joan S. Stark, Malcolm A. Lowther, *Strengthening the Ties That Bind, Integrating Undergraduate Liberal and Professional Study, Report of the Professional Preparation Network.*

The Professional Preparation Project of the Center for the Study of Higher and Postsecondary Education of the University of Michigan has undertaken an ambitious *Professional/Liberal Undergraduate Self-Study PLUSS* and developed an interesting and instructive questionnaire.

See also the report prepared at Samuel Neaman Institute of the Technion in Haifa, "Engineering Education 2001," *Engineering Education* (November 1987): 106–24, 113ff.

Engineering Undergraduate Education, Panel on Undergraduate Engineering Education (E. T. Cranch, Chairman), Committee on Education and Utilization of the Engineer, is an important general report.

Samuel C. Florman's thoughtful and well-written book *The Civilized Engineer* should be read by anyone interested in our subject.

1. Speaking One's Mind

1. See Ernest Boyer, *College: The Undergraduate Experience in America,* 101.

2. The notable exceptions are, of course, Presidents Hoover and Carter. Governor John Sununu is also an engineer.

3. See also Samuel C. Florman, *The Civilized Engineer,* 178.

2. A Manly Profession

1. For the social theorists concerned with the human implications of scientific and technological change see Sanford A. Lakoff, "The Third Culture," *Knowledge and Power*, 1–61.

2. That antagonism would be replaced by productive cooperation and peaceful order in an industrial society guided by science (i.e., by scientists) was one of the tenets of Henri de Saint-Simon, whose followers were chiefly responsible for the building of the Suez Canal. The opening of the canal in 1869 moved Theodor Herzl, among others, to seek to do as much, in the same Saint-Simonian spirit, in Panama, whereas Whitman was inspired to celebrate the "Year of the marriage, of continents, climates and oceans" in *Passage to India*. See D. A. Farnie, *East and West of Suez*, 91.

Alfred Nobel, whose Peace Prize was intended to honor those who contributed to achieving fraternity among nations, abolishing or reducing standing armies, or organizing peace conferences is reputed to have remarked to Bertha von Suttner, who had been his secretary and was an ardent and active pacifist—and who received the Nobel Peace Prize in 1905—that his invention of dynamite would bring peace to the world sooner than her rallies.

3. I understand that Harvey Mudd College, one of the finest engineering schools in the country, which has always prided itself in providing its students with an education, not just technical training, is currently under pressure from ABET (the accreditation authority) to *restrict* the general humanities and social science part of the curriculum.

4. *Engineering News* (May 4, 1893):445.

5. *Engineering News and American Contract Journal* (October 16, 1886):513, 249.

6. For the different nuances in the development of these schools see Earl F. Cheit, *The Useful Arts and the Liberal Tradition*.

7. Ibid., 1, 2.

8. Dartmouth, with its Thayer School, is a notable exception.

9. Alfred, Lord Tennyson, "Mechanophilus" (ca. 1833). Compare also a draft, not included by Tennyson in the published version of this poem:

> Away with shadows! Render all
> Plain, palpable and bold
> Then give the crude material
> that we may carve and mold.

10. *The Technology Review* (May 1911):310.

3. Second Thoughts: The Needs of Advanced Industrial Societies

1. Alfred North Whitehead, "The Place of Classics in Education," in *The Aims of Education and Other Essays*, 94.

2. *Novum Organum*, Aphorism III.

3. Daniel Bell, *The Coming of Post-Industrial Society: A Venture in Social Forecasting*. New York, 1973.

4. Failure to adjust the educational system to the functional needs of development is a sign and itself one of the causes of underdevelopment. The problems connected with the betrayed aspirations of "overqualified" underemployed graduates in ostensibly "high prestige" fields together with the dearth of people possessing the skills to do the job at hand are too well known to be elaborated on here.

5. The truth is that recruiters who have to satisfy the needs of operations with limited budgets and restricted objectives will not look for the same graduates that their own CEO's, taking a longer view, would prefer. The problem is structural and can only be overcome by shrewd advisers.

6. Earl F. Cheit, *The Useful Arts and the Liberal Tradition,* 95.

7. *Encyclopaedia Britannica,* 11th edition, s.v., "Education." This statement about the needs of industry fodder is followed by a confident statement of the democratic impact of this development, undimmed by the spectre of the great industrialized totalitarianisms that were to mark the following half-century: "Politically . . . increasing demonstrations of institutions renders a wide diffusion of knowledge and the cultivation of a high standard of intelligence among the people a necessary precaution of prudent statesmanship."

8. See the admirably concise study of the problems of transition in higher education by Martin Trow, "Problems in the Transition from Elite to Mass Higher Education," in *Policies for Higher Education,* 55–101.

4. *Literacy and Democracy*

1. Report of the Andrew W. Mellon Foundation, 1988, 15, 16.

2. Ernest Gellner, *Nations & Nationalism,* 28.

3. Ibid., 24, 25.

5. *Technology and Freedom*

1. According to Gellner, the dominant, indispensable means of social control in modern societies is what he calls the "universal Danegeld," alluding to the tribute paid by the Britons to keep the Danes from engaging in massacre and plunder, "buying off social aggression with material enhancement. Its greatest weakness is its inability to survive any temporary reduction of the social bribery fund and to weather the loss of legitimacy which befalls it if the cornucopia becomes temporarily jammed and the flow falters" (Ernest Gellner, *Nations & Nationalism,* 22).

2. For the ways in which the educational system becomes not only a means to provide for but a manner of paying out the "Danegeld," the extent to which it serves as an instrument of social policy equivalent to social security and other more direct practices of redistribution for the sake of social stability, see Peter Flora and Arnold J. Heidenheimer, eds., *The Development of Welfare States in Europe and America,* and in particular chap. 8, by Heidenheimer in "Education and Social Security Entitlements in Europe and America":

> For the society as a whole, however, perhaps the most significant difference between the institutional bases of the welfare state in Great Britain and the United States was the emphasis placed on public education — especially for lower income groups in the United States. Massive support for the expansion of public education, including higher education in the United States, must be seen as a central component of the American notion of welfare — the idea that through public education both personal betterment and national social and economic development would take place.' . . . It was in (the 1880's) that Britain, Germany and the United States all came to combine mass enfranchisement with the bureaucratic potential for policy steering and implementation in rapidly industrializing systems. . . . We can perceive the three countries selecting alternative governmental responses to the need and demands for equality and security. . . . Germany gave priority to meeting secu-

rity needs to the lower classes by introducing compulsory insurance programs. The United States responded more to equality demands by enhancing mobility opportunities for individuals through the initiation of an unprecedented expansion of postprimary education opportunities, largely through state and local governments. Germany used its expanded social security system to deflect upward mobility ambitions, and imposed a system of 'tight coupling' between its educational, labor market and social security systems. The United States continued a strategy of 'substituting education for techniques of social action' and encouraged a system of 'loose coupling' which accommodated more varied meritocratic accumulation tactics by individuals. . . . Ideological proclivities, of course, played a role in deciding these choices. But there are also important structural reasons that foreclosed the other choices at this time. (274–75)

One of the keys to the historically different pattern of development is whether powerful bureaucracies were built as social-control mechanisms before or after the development of political parties as instruments of influence pursuing the advancement of social groups (270).

3. Robert M. White, "Of Walls and Bridges," *The Bridge* 19, no. 4 (Winter 1989–Spring 1990): 2–3.

4. The idea of the interests taming the passions is, of course, not new. See Albert O. Hirschman, *The Passions and the Interests: Political Arguments for Capitalism Before Its Triumph*.

5. Truman had kept the poem in his pocket since graduation, recopying it twenty or thirty times as the paper wore out! Merle Miller, *Plain Speaking: An Oral Biography of Harry S Truman*, 428–29.

6. *Efficiency vs. the Love of One's Own*

1. John F. Welch, Jr., "Engineering and the Discipline of the Marketplace," *The Bridge* 18, no. 4 (Winter 1988): 2.

2. He recommends, in fact, lower capital gains taxes, lower interest rates, R&D credit, education, and trade policies "that insist on free global markets."

That other nations have done "quite well" is, of course, an understatement, if one considers the most spectacularly successful economies, Germany and Japan, both apparently benefiting from intelligent—that is cautious rather than wholesale—social-democratic interventionism.

7. *Cultural Literacy*

1. See Pierre Bourdieu and Jean-Claude Passeron, *The Inheritors: French Students and Their Relation to Culture*. The educational and social situation in France is different in many important respects from that in the U.S. Nevertheless, whatever one may think about the authors' broader thesis regarding the sociology of cultural reproduction as a dimension of social reproduction, the book contains important insights on the differential reception of academic language and culture.

2. In response to a story in the *New York Times* about the history books recently adopted in California, which present, among other things, different kinds of bread brought to America by immigrants from different countries, one forward-looking correspondent writes, "Why not dispense with texts of history and let the student's own backgrounds provide the text? A project on diversity, allowing children in California and elsewhere to build on their own history, would be more

conducive to learning than reading a text. Just think, the students could bring in their own bread and eat it together" (*New York Times Magazine,* Oct. 20, 1991, 12). An amazingly shallow notion of culture makes it possible to imagine that "backgrounds" speak for themselves and are immediately intelligible to each other. One wonders, besides, how many children, regardless of "background," are likely to bring Wonder-Bread to school.

3. Frederick Mosteller, Daniel Patrick Moynihan, eds., *On Equality of Educational Opportunity,* Papers deriving from the Harvard University Faculty Seminar on the Coleman Report.

More recently Daniel Patrick Moynihan, "Educational Goals and Political Plans," *Public Interest* (Winter 1991): 32–48.

4. E. D. Hirsch, Jr., *Cultural Literacy: What Every American Needs to Know.* Hirsch is also the moving force behind the Cultural Literacy Foundation, 2012–B Morton Drive, Charlottesville, VA, 22901.

5. T. S. Eliot, *Notes Towards the Definition of Culture.*

6. Hirsch, *Cultural Literacy,* xii.

7. Mario Vargas-Llosa, answering a question following a presentation he made at the University of Colorado about the preservation of indigenous Indian cultures in his native Peru, pointed out the delicacy of the matter. The respect and love for the traditional and particular can become a self-righteous expression of the discontent of those living in industrial society and can involve the presumption of choosing "what is best" for the indigenous cultures for them, excluding them from the benefits—with all their drawbacks—of modern society. It comes down to "you stay poor because I like you to remain picturesque."

8. Of Content and Form in Teaching

1. See C. D. Kingsley, ed. *Cardinal Principles of Secondary Education: A Report of the Commission on the Reorganization of Secondary Education.*

2. See E. D. Hirsch, Jr., *Cultural Literacy: What Every American Needs to Know,* 123. For a major critique of the shortcomings of "progressive" education and its unwitting betrayal of democratic aspirations see: Arthur Bestor, *The Restoration of Learning.*

9. The Tower of Babel

1. E. D. Hirsch, Jr., *Cultural Literacy: What Every American Needs to Know,* 2.

2. Gen., 10:11.

3. The standard reference is to Robert Bellah, "Civil Religion in America," in *Religion in America,* ed. W. G. McLoughlin and R. Bellah, 3–23. See also Russel E. Richey, Donald G. Jones, eds., *American Civil Religion.* For a philosophically articulated, ontologically open view of civil religion, see Eric Voegelin, *The New Science of Politics.*

4. Hirsch, *Cultural Literarcy,* 96.

5. Ibid., 96

6. Ibid., 99.

7. Ernest Gellner, *Nations & Nationalism,* 56.

8. See Sanford A. Lakoff, "Schools and Democratic Values," *American Educator* (Summer 1981):15–19, who concludes, "When it comes to the role of the schools in inculcating democratic values, the standard is the same as in all other aspects of academic instruction: education, yes; indoctrination, no!"

10. E Pluribus Unum?

1. See Bruce Ackerman, *Social Justice in the Liberal State*. Jennifer L. Hochshild, *What's Fair? American Beliefs About Distributive Justice*.

2. Aristotle, *Politics*, II, 3, 1261a.

3. See Harvey C. Mansfield, Jr., *America's Constitutional Soul*, 11.

4. David Schneider, *American Kinship*, quoted by Talcott Parsons, "Change of Ethnicity," in *Ethnicity*, edited by Nathan Glazer and Daniel Patrick Moynihan, 65.

11. Diversity and Its Discontents

1. *The Liberties of the Massachusetts Collonie in New England, of 1641*, art. 94, 8. (deriving from Leviticus 24:15, 11.)

2. See the First and Fifth amendments to the U.S. Constitution.

3. The difficulty of recognizing and admitting how great the difference from the other can be is easily underestimated by people of good will. At the European University Institute in Florence, which draws students and staff from the twelve countries of the European Community and beyond, I had the opportunity to observe the following phenomenon: people from the various countries, who were, by means of their self-selection, clearly disposed to live and work in what was, for all but the Italians, a foreign country and to mix and work with people of different nationalities found it, in fact, in an extraordinary number of cases, very difficult to adjust. They (I should say we) were *expecting* to find differences, but the differences we actually encountered were not the ones we expected. The *realms* in which we were disposed to be tolerant and understanding, indeed welcoming of differences, were not coterminous, even within the relatively narrow compass of Western European civilization. The opposite is also true: that one cherishes as specifically one's own cultural expressions that are, in fact, broadly shared. A worldly industrialist and respected civic leader, watching an American college football game, pointing to the half-time performance, remarked with pride, "If only those Russians and Eastern Europeans could see this!" What he expected these deprived people to admire was precisely what is most like the youth group displays of socialist countries.

12. "O! that the Everlasting had not fix'd His canon 'gainst self-slaughter!"

1. That is, I believe, the number of titles on the notorious Stanford ex-Western Civilization course.

2. Benjamin Barber, "The Civic Mission of the University," *Kettering Review* (Fall 1989):64.

3. Robert M. Hutchins, *The Great Conversation: The Substance of a Liberal Education*, xvii.

4. Sterne and Fielding have, in fact, been dropped from the latest (1990) edition of the *Britannica Great Books*.

5. Moses I. Finley, "Crisis in the Classics," *Crisis in the Humanities*, ed. J. H. Plumb, 11–23, 14, 15.

13. Innocents Abroad

1. George Kennan, "The Future of Professional Diplomacy," *Foreign Affairs* 33 (1954–1955): 566–67.

2. See Henry M. Wriston, "Young Men in the Foreign Service," *Foreign Affairs* 33 (1954–1955): 28.

3. Theodore C. Sorenson, "America's First Post–Cold War President" *Foreign Affairs* (Fall 1992): 14.

4. There are remarkable exceptions: Worcester Polytechnic seems to have an exemplary program of overseas study for engineers. See Lance Schachterle, "WPI in the World: The WPI Global Project Program" *Interactions,* 10:11f.

14. Manifest Destiny vs. the Serpent Columbus

1. See, for example, the celebration of Columbus by Samuel Morison, *Admiral of the Ocean Sea: A Life of Christopher Columbus.*

2. Descartes, Prefatory letter to *Principes de la Philosophie,* Adam-Tannery, vol. 9, 2, 14f.

3. See Carlo Cipolla's admirably balanced and charmingly written *Guns, Sails and Empires: Technological Innovation and European Expansion 1400–1700.*

4. See, for example, Kirkpatrick Sale, *The Conquest of Paradise;* or Howard Zinn, *The People's History of the United States.*

15. Babylonian Captivity and the Suffering Servant

1. "On Cannibals," in *The Complete Essays of Montaigne,* transl. D. Frame, no. 31, 152. It is interesting to note that Montaigne collected artifacts of natives of America and appreciated their poetry, an example of which he calls "Anacreontic" (158). He did not fail to see that once they had come into contact with Europeans, their "desire for new things" would be their ruin.

2. Ibid., 156.

3. Karl Marx and Friedrich Engels, *The Communist Manifesto,* 26.

4. Ibid, 19.

5. Ibid, 26.

6. Isa., 40ff. Isaiah characteristically envisages a levelling process: "Every valley shall be exalted and every mountain and hill shall be made low: and the crooked shall be made straight and the rough places plain" (40:4).

7. Marx, *Communist Manifesto,* 21.

8. Ibid., 20.

9. Ibid., 13.

10. Ibid., 13.

11. Frantz Fanon, *The Wretched of the Earth.* The English translation of the title loses the poignancy of the French participle, which suggests a condemnation and evokes hell.

16. Separation as Collective Therapy

1. Charles Junkerman, Assistant Dean of Undergraduate Studies at Stanford, answering criticism of the new CIV course in the *Wall Street Journal,* wrote,

> For example, 50 years ago John Locke seemed indispensable in answering a question like "What is social justice?" In 1989 with a more interdependent world order, a more heterogenous domestic population and mass media and communication systems that complicate our definitions of "society" and "individual." It may be that someone like Frantz Fanon, a black Algerian psychoanalyst, will get us closer to the answer we need. (January 6, 1989)

Junkerman's statement begs every conceivable question: whether justice is merely a function of "the times," whether the change in the last fifty years is so immeasurably greater than that between the time when Locke wrote and World War II, whether the color of an author's skin and the location of his adopted country guarantees the pertinence and cogency of his discourse, etc. If pertinence is so transient, why waste any time on what is here today and gone tomorrow?

In virtue of what, finally, do we opt for presentism? Is the criterion itself immune to time, or is this verity alone exempt from the iron rule of obsolescence? At what intervals is humanity reborn as a different species so that we cannot learn from the past?

2. He has changed his name to Kwame Ture, presumably in recognition of both Ghana's Kwame Nkrumah and Guinea's Sekou Touré.

3. See Robert Penn Warren, *Who Speaks for the Negro?*, 390ff.

4. See Frantz Fanon, *Black Skin, White Masks*.

5. Jean-Paul Sartre, *Reflexions Sur la Question Juive*. Sartre is, in turn, indebted to the rather more complex discussion of the ostensible relation of capitalism and class conflict not only to the hatred of Jews but to Jewishness itself in Karl Marx, *On The Jewish Question*, in *Early Writings*, ed. T. B. Bottomore, 3–40.

6. With regard to actual practices in traditional African societies see, for instance, Edward Evan Evans-Pritchard, *Azande: History and Political Institutions*.

17. The Crustacean Theory of Culture

1. Note Cleaver's remarkable classification of alienated, universally frustrated humanity into white male "Omnipotent Administrators," unable to satisfy the cravings of white "Ultrafeminine Dolls," "Supermasculine Menial" blacks, who, being deprived of their minds by the Administrators, are held in contempt by black "Amazons" who defer instead to the authority of omnipotent Administrators. Eldridge Cleaver, "The Primeval Mitosis," *Soul on Ice*, 176–90. "The Class Society projects a fragmented sexual image. . . . The people within that society are motivated and driven, by the perennial quest for Apocalyptic Fusion, to achieve this highest identity, or as close as they can come to the perfection of the Unitary Sexual Image" (178). In the meanwhile, misogyny is a concomitant of this mode of achieving "recognition."

2. See Arend Lijphart, *Democracy in Plural Societies*, or his more recent *Democracies: Patterns of Majoritarian and Consensus Government in Twenty-One Countries*. With specific reference to South Africa see also Donald L. Horowitz, *A Democratic South Africa? Constitutional Engineering in a Divided Society*. "Devolution" is much discussed in Britain, and autonomous regions have been established in Spain and Italy, for instance, in order to accommodate historical and sociocultural disparities. Whether decentralization leads to a greater degree of harmony or proves instead to be the thin end of the wedge of dissolution (as in Yugoslavia and Czechoslovakia) depends on the particular circumstances of the case.

3. Alexander Hamilton, James Madison, John Jay, *The Federalist*, no. 15.

4. Lewis Carroll, *Through the Looking Glass*, 6.

5. See George Orwell, *1984*, and "Politics and the English Language," in *The Collected Essays, Journalism and Letters of George Orwell*, vol. 4, *In Front of Your Nose, 1945–1950*, ed. Sonia Orwell and Ian Angus, no. 38, 127–40.

6. Niccolo Machiavelli, *The Prince*, chap. 15.

7. See Michael Naumann, *Der Abbau einer Verkehrten Welt*.

8. Sometimes *strictly* mechanical, as in the software programs for editing textbooks, etc. My own college, in a burst of humorless conformism, changed the sign honoring the recipients of the "Distinguished Engineering Alumnus Awards" to "Distinguished Engineering Alumni Award," in the mystifying belief that the masculine plural is less sexist than the masculine singular, thus achieving both bad grammar and continued political incorrectness.

18. Herstory?

1. The choice of Cleopatra due, no doubt, to Hollywood having made her name familiar to the great public, is particularly, perhaps characteristically, bizarre. The last of the Ptolemies, she came from a Macedonian family who had hardly ever married outside the family for some three hundred years!

19. Conformity and Individuality

1. Lawrence Durrell, *Justine,* 14. Durrell adds, "You would never mistake it for a happy place." Alexandria was also, characteristically for a certain mode of diversity, not a society of citizens, but of subjects and resident aliens. Participatory republics seem to encourage, as they require, a common ethos.

2. John Stuart Mill, *On Liberty,* chap. 3, in J. S. Mill, *Utilitarianism, Liberty and Representative Government,* ed. E. Rhys, 126.

3. Ibid., 125.

4. George Levine, Peter Brooks, et al. *Speaking for the Humanities,* American Council of Learned Societies, 1989, Occasional Paper, no. 7, 6.

5. Lou Robinson, "Disdain false democracy" *American Book Review* (October–November 1991):1, 11.

6. Mill, *On Liberty,* 120–21.

20. What Is the Tower of Babel For?

1. Václav Havel, *Disturbing the Peace,* 14.

2. Max Weber, *The Protestant Ethic and the Spirit of Capitalism,* transl. Talcott Parsons, 181.

3. Ibid., 182.

4. The notion of "modern project," popularized for the American academic public in a critical spirit by the late Leo Strauss is, of course, a historically circumscribed version of what Heidegger took to be a universal human *Ent-wurf.*

5. Giambattista Vico, *On the Study Method of Our Time,* transl. Elias Gianturco, 93. (I have departed from Gianturco's translation in minor points of nuance, mainly to avoid archaisms.)

6. See chap. 3 of this book.

7. C. P. Snow, *The Two Cultures; and a Second Look.*

21. A Scientific Morality?

1. See Jacques Barzun, *Science: The Glorious Entertainment.*

2. Linus Pauling, "Scientists in Politics," in *The Place of Values in a World of Facts,* Proceedings of the Fourteenth Nobel Symposium, September 15–20, 1969, ed. A. Tiselins, S. Nilsson, 197–205, 201.

3. Opinions differ, of course, as to how successful OTA has been. Criticism is mainly directed at the apparent weakness of the office in recruiting and retaining scientists and technology experts of the highest order. To the degree that such

criticism is valid, it must be seen in the context of the historical and structural weakness of the American Civil Service as a whole.

4. It is worth noting of the two engineers to be elected President of the United States, one, Herbert Hoover, was also a very able Latinist. Whether the misfortunes of his presidency can be put down to his engineering or to his Latin or to other causes independent of his education is, of course, difficult to decide.

5. Celestine V, a saintly hermit elected pope in 1294, found it impossible to reconcile the exercise of power with the purity of his conscience and abdicated within four months, making room for the ruthless Boniface VIII. Dante, consequently, put Celestine in hell (*Inferno,* 3, 60: "who made, for cowardice, the great refusal"). Had he lived long enough, Dante would no doubt have created a special infernal circle for scientists indulging in the politics of clean hands and another one, lower down, for those who seek to impose "scientific" solutions to problems of value.

6. The prestige of the businessman is especially great in America. There are good historical reasons for this: in relation to Continental Europe or China, for example, the state was not highly developed, its service conferred little advantage or honor. The social mobility made possible by an ever-expanding frontier made the accumulation of commensurable goods (money), rather than differentiation in terms of incommensurable goods such as rank, family ties, military, and ecclesiastical or administrative preferment, the decisive criterion of social status to an even greater degree than was the case elsewhere. The development of the vast resources of the country promised a better avenue to both wealth and prestige than (explicit) links to government, and therefore naturally attracted the best talents. The businessman's competence thus became a self-realizing proposition.

This is very different from countries in which, at any rate by now, careers are equally open to talent, but in which patterns of prestige have been created by a different historical experience, so that top French business cadres, for example, are (or were until recently) drawn from a highly esteemed and competent civil service rather than the other way around.

None of this changes the fundamental problem of mistaking politics for administration and technical competence for sound judgment.

22. *Two Cultures?*

1. C. P. Snow, *The Two Cultures,* 11. Later, in *A Second Look,* Snow spoke of a "Third Culture," encompassing social scientists concerned with "how human beings live in terms of fact, not legend," a culture in which the other two might be reconciled. Sanford A. Lakoff's article "The Third Culture" borrows the title but adopts a rather different spirit. Note Snow's unyielding scientistic bias expressed in the contrast "fact"—"legend," and the continued mistaking of modes of understanding for fields of knowledge. F. R. Leavis unleashed a critical attack on Snow, which raises many of the pertinent issues but whose value is diminished by the virulent personal tone in which he chose to deliver it. F. R. Leavis, *Two Cultures? The Significance of C. P. Snow,* with an essay on Sir Charles Snow's Rede Lecture by Michael Judkins.

2. Ibid., 27, 50.

3. Ibid., 51.

4. The first British Prime Minister to have a degree in science did not come to office until twenty years after Snow's lecture: Mrs. Thatcher.

5. Ibid., 5. Snow's Rede Lecture was delivered, it will be remembered, not long after the coronation of Queen Elizabeth II.

6. Ibid., 16.

7. Ibid., 13.

8. Ibid., 6.

9. Ibid., 7.

10. The point is, of course, made by T. S. Eliot:

The élites, in consequence, will consist solely of individuals whose only common bond will be their professional interest: with no social cohesion, with no social continuity. They will be united only by a part, and that the most conscious part, of their personalities; they will meet like committees. The greater part of their "culture" will be only what they share with all the other individuals composing their nation. (*Notes Towards the Definition of Culture,* 47)

11. Snow, *Two Cultures,* 10, 11.

23. The Retreat from the Word

1. See George Steiner, "The Retreat from the Word," in *Language and Silence.*

2. Ibid., 34.

3. Quoted in *Chronicle of Higher Education,* May 9, 1990.

4. Alfred North Whitehead, "The Rhythmic Claims of Freedom and Discipline," in *The Aims of Education and Other Essays,* 45–65, 45–46.

5. See Michael Oakeshott, "The Study of 'Politics' in a University" in *Rationalism in Politics,* 184–218. And see Timothy Fuller, ed., *The Voice of Liberal Learning: Michael Oakeshott on Education.*

6. What makes an education liberal is not "the mere inclusion of arts subjects. Both science and arts subjects can be passed on by liberal or illiberal procedures. Literature and science can both be treated as 'subjects' and, as it were, stamped in on the students. Or—treated as living disciplines of critical thought and of the imagination, in short, students can be trained on an apprenticeship system" (Richard Starky Peters, "Must An Education Have An Aim?" in Charles James Baez Macmillan and Thomas W. Nelson, eds. *Concepts of Teaching: Philosophical Essays,* 94).

7. Since so many people have come to rely on these devices, the invention of "context sensitive" spellcheckers leads to a true improvement of the writing, though hardly of the writers. The older types of machine did not pick up errors due to the use of perfectly good words, that just happened to be the wrong ones, e.g., "I would of gone . . . ," found in countless student papers.

8. Kiku Adatto, "The Incredible Shrinking Sound Bite," *New Republic* (May 28, 1990):20.

9. Steiner, "Retreat from the Word," 25.

24. Teaching Values

1. *The Existential Pleasures of Engineering.* The strength but also the moral ambiguities of the "existential" character of technical enterprises is well dramatized by *The Bridge on the River Kwai.*

2. Aristotle's *Politics* is characteristically ambiguous in this respect. Machiavelli's "how-to" book—*The Prince*—but also modern books on *Who Gets*

What, When, How (the title of Harold Lasswell's well-known book) illustrate my point.

3. Aristotle, *Politics,* VIII, ii, 1337a-1377d., transl. E. Barker, 333–34.

4. John Milton, *Tractate on Education,* ed. Oscar Browning, 3.

5. Mark Van Doren, "Nobody Thinks He Is Educated," in *Liberal Education,* 1f.

25. Courses of Study

1. See ch. 16, n. 1, *Gorgias,* 480b. See also *Republic,* II, 362e f.

2. So-called 3/2 programs provide for a combined or double degree in Arts and Engineering obtainable in five years. They may allow some scope for liberal studies before the student focuses on a discipline—but they also frequently tend to degenerate in the direction of vocationalism.

26. Humanist Education

1. See Anthony Grafton and Lisa Jardine, *From Humanism to the Humanities.*

2. See the admirable chapter on the education of women in Grafton and Jardine. In the education of Renaissance women of high birth, who are, in principle, excluded from the conduct of public affairs, considerations of utility are excluded *ex hypothesi* and one might say to a fault. As with the "accomplishments" of Victorian girls, it is not easy to discern how much of this is liberal, how much is exclusionary, and how much is socially, i.e., indirectly useful.

3. Moses Hadas, *Old Wine, New Bottles: A Humanist Teacher at Work,* 14.

27. The Civic Mission of the University

1. Benjamin Barber, "The Civic Mission of the University, " *Kettering Review* (Fall 1989):67.

2. Robert Maynard Hutchins, *The Great Conversation: The Substance of a Liberal Education,* xv, 17ff.

3. Barber, "Civic Mission," 68.

4. Ibid.

5. Ibid., 66.

6. Ralf Dahrendorf, *Essays in the Theory of Society,* 167.

7. Ibid., 177–78.

8. Barber, "Civic Mission," 68.

28. Opportunities and Constraints

1. See the recommendations, for instance, in *Colorado Engineer* (Fall 1989):16.

2. Edwin S. Burdell et al., *General Education in Engineering,* Report of the Humanistic-Social Research Project, American Society for Engineering Education, 34.

3. Strengthening liberal content is one of the stated purposes of engineering colleges set on maintaining and improving their standards, including CU. See College of Engineering and Applied Science, University of Colorado, Boulder, *A Strategic Plan,* December 1986.

4. Edwin J. Holstein and Earl D. McGrath, *Liberal Education and Engineering,* 54.

5. Joseph S. Johnston, Jr. et al, *Unfinished Design: The Humanities and Social Sciences in Undergraduate Engineering Education,* 7.

6. Burdell, *General Education,* 18.

7. See Johnston, *Unfinished Design,* 11.

8. Holstein and McGrath, *Liberal Education,* 65.

9. Burdell, *General Education,* 21, 29; Samuel C. Florman, *The Civilized Engineer,* 210–11.

10. Sterling P. Olmstead et al., *Liberal Learning for the Engineer,* 13; see also Burdell, *General Education,* 21.

11. Olmstead, *Liberal Learning,* 14.

12. Burdell, *General Education,* 37.

13. The University of Virginia is a case in point. Pedagogical focus is given by the senior thesis prepared by students under the supervision of two advisers, one technical, the other a "humanist." See S. S. Fisher, E. L. Gaden, O. A. Gianniny, Jr., L. A. Hoel, *Future Alternatives with Respect to the Division of Humanities in the School of Engineering and Applied Science* (brochure), Charlottesville, VA, April 1984. I am very grateful to the Dept. of Humanities in the School of Engineering at UVA for allowing me to visit and have conversations with most of the faculty from whom I learned a great deal.

29. The Text-Based Seminar

1. Sterling P. Olmstead et al., *Liberal Learning for the Engineer,* 17.

2. Joseph S. Johnston, Jr. et al., *Unfinished Design: The Humanities and Social Sciences in Undergraduate Engineering,* chap. 4.

3. Edwin S. Burdell et al., *General Education in Engineering,* Report of the Humanistic-Social Research Project, 16.

4. Ibid., 16, 11.

5. Themes that may not be appropriate to discussion classes are, however, appropriate to other formats, such as public lectures, etc., which students should be encouraged to attend.

6. For a reasoned account of the syllabus, the pedagogic reasons for the choice and order of the readings, and the exercises that go with them see Leland Giovannelli, "Teaching Students How to Think for Themselves," in American Society for Engineering Education Proceedings, 1991, 2008–14. This paper is available from the University of Colorado, College of Engineering, Campus Box 422, Boulder, CO, 80309–0422. The following table gives an idea of a "pedagogic" arrangement of offerings as adopted by the Herbst Program at CU.

Schematic Table of Seminar Offerings

Readings	Skills			Writing			
	"Social"	"Reading"		Skills	Types (genre) of writing		
	(Distinguish?)						
I. Narrative	Community building	Attention to text / What *it* says	CLASSROOM TECHNIQUES	Diction—Syntax / What do my words say?	Abstracts	EXERCISES IN WRITING	TUTORIAL CONFERENCES
II. Dramatic	Suspending judgment / Role-playing / "Form"	Authors / Characters / Context / Adducing evidence		Poetic analysis / Craftsmanship / Arguing from evidence / Attention to dramatic form	"Essays"		
III. Analytical	Elements of analysis / Principles—reasons / Intellectual rigor / Uncovering unstated premises & tacitly assumed principles			Logical analysis / Attention to structuring argument / Spotting fallacies	Expository		
IV. Self-examining	How does it speak to *me*? / What about the *me* that responds in this way?			Form & content / Personal voice / Longer, sustained argument			

7. Hence the apt name of a remarkable project, which seeks to introduce discussion classes in schools, especially disadvantaged schools: *The Touchstone Project,* CZM, 6 N. Cherry Grove Ave., Annapolis, MD, 21401. I have benefited a great deal from the formal expositions and even more from conversations with the initiators of that project.

A Last Word

1. Samuel C. Florman, *The Civilized Engineer* 34f, 58. As to the disputed nature of the relative dignity of the pure vs. the applied sciences, one need only visit with the several departments of a modern university to see that the matter is far from settled. The intriguing and difficult question, why premodern societies—China and India, for example, as well as Ancient Greece—resisted translating scientific knowledge into technological applications cannot be adequately answered by pointing to the snobbery of a handful of thinkers.

2. Homer, *Odyssey,* xxix, 189; xix, 138f.

3. Homer, *Iliad,* 6, 454–58.

4. On the affirmation of the ordinary, etc., see Charles Taylor, *Sources of the Self.* A recent exaltation of the dignity of labor, more perhaps—and, some would say, disturbingly so—than the dignity of the laborer, is to be found in Pope John-Paul II's encyclica *Laborem Exercens.*

5. See A. Moulakis, "The Value of Work," in *Sophia and Praxis: The Boundaries of Politics,* ed. Jene Porter, 129f.

6. Frederick Douglass. *Narrative of the Life of Frederick Douglass: An American Slave, Written by Himself.*

7. Aristotle, *Politics,* I, iv, 1253b.

8. See Hannah Arendt, *The Human Condition. Who* will be compelled that others may be free is, by contrast, a social matter.

9. Samuel C. Florman, *The Existential Pleasures of Engineering;* see also, the chapter of the same name in Florman, *The Civilized Engineer,* 18f.

10. Florman, *Existential Pleasures.* The Parthenon did, in fact, also serve as a treasury of the Athenian League, but it is in this regard infinitely less admirable than Fort Knox.

11. Ibid.

12. Ibid., 34–35.

13. Sophocles, *Antigone,* 332–72.

14. Ibid., 368.

15. Gen., 1:3.

16. A diacritical dot on the *b* or *v* (depending precisely on the dot) makes it possible to distinguish between the two meanings, but that would seem to be a late development—certainly after the Fall!

17. Johann Wolfgang von Goethe, *Faust,* part 1, "Faust's Study," l. 1224–37, transl. C. F. MacIntyre, in *A Treasury of the Theatre,* ed. John Gassner, 516.

18. Thomas Aquinas, *Commentary on the Sentences,* 2d. 15, 3, 3. Quoted in Josef Pieper, *Leisure: The Basis of Culture,* 67.

Works Cited

Ackerman, Bruce. *Social Justice in the Liberal State*. New Haven, Conn.: Yale University Press, 1980.

Adatto, Kiku. "The Incredible Shrinking Sound Bite." *New Republic* (May 28, 1990):20

Aquinas, Thomas. *Commentary on the Sentences*. Quoted in Josef Pieper. *Leisure: The Basis of Culture*. New York: New American Library, 1963.

Arendt, Hannah. *The Human Condition*. Chicago: University of Chicago Press, 1958

Aristotle. *Politics*. Translated by E. Barker. London: Oxford University Press, 1946.

Association of American Colleges. *An Engineering Student's Guide to the Humanities and Social Sciences*, Washington, D.C.: 1988.

Bacon, Francis. *Novum Organum*, edited by Thomas Fowler. Oxford: Clarendon Press, 1878.

Barber, Benjamin. "The Civic Mission of the University." *Kettering Review* (Fall 1989):62–72.

Barzun, Jacques. *Science: The Glorious Entertainment*. New York: Harper & Row, 1964.

Bell, Daniel. *The Coming of Post-Industrial Society: A Venture in Social Forecasting*. New York: Basic Books, 1973.

Bellah, Robert. "Civil Religion in America." In *Religion in America*, edited by William Gerald McLoughlin and Robert N. Bellah. Boston: Houghton Mifflin, 1968, 3–23.

Bellamy, Edward. *Looking Backward, 2000–1887*. Boston: Houghton Mifflin, 1889.

Bestor, Arthur. *The Restoration of Learning*. New York: Knopf, 1955.

Bourdieu, Pierre, Jean-Claude Passeron. *The Inheritors: French Students and Their Relation to Culture*. Chicago: University of Chicago Press, 1979.

Boyer, Ernest. *College: The Undergraduate Experience in America*. New York: Harper & Row, 1987.

Burdell, Edwin S., et al. *General Education in Engineering: A Report of the Humanistic-Social Research Project.* Washington, D.C.: American Society of Engineering Educators, 1956.

Carroll, Lewis. *Through the Looking Glass.* In *The Annotated Alice.* Cleveland: World Publishing, 1963.

Cheit, Earl F. *The Useful Arts and the Liberal Tradition.* New York: McGraw Hill and Carnegie Foundation, 1975.

Chronicle of Higher Education. May 9, 1990.

Cipolla, Carlo. *Guns, Sails and Empires: Technological Innovation and European Expansion 1400–1700.* London: Collins, 1965.

Cleaver, Eldridge. *Soul on Ice.* New York: Delta, 1968.

College of Engineering and Applied Science, University of Colorado, Boulder. *A Strategic Plan.* December 1986.

College of Engineering and Applied Science, University of Colorado, Boulder. *The Colorado Engineer.* Fall 1989.

Dahrendorf, Ralf. *Essays in the Theory of Society.* Stanford: Stanford University Press, 1968.

Descartes, René. *Principes de la Philosophie.* In *Oeuvres de Descartes,* edited by Charles Adam and Paul Tannery. Paris: Cerf, 1904, 9:2.

Douglass, Frederick. *Narrative of the Life of Frederick Douglass, An American Slave, Written by Himself.* Boston: Anti-Slavery Office, 1846. Reprint. New York: Doubleday, 1983.

Durrell, Lawrence. *Justine.* New York: Dutton, 1957.

"Education." In *Encyclopaedia Britannica.* 11th edition. Cambridge: Cambridge University Press, 1910.

Eliot, T. S. *Notes Towards the Definition of Culture.* New York: Harcourt Brace, 1949. Reprint. London: Faber, 1962.

Engineering News and American Contract Journal. October 16, 1886.

Engineering News and Railroad Journal. February 3, 1893.

Evans-Pritchard, Edward Evan. *Azande: History and Political Institutions.* Oxford: Clarendon Press, 1971.

Fanon, Frantz. *Black Skin, White Masks.* New York: Grove Press, 1967.

———. *The Wretched of the Earth.* New York: Grove Press, 1966.

Farnie, D. A. *East and West of Suez.* Oxford: Oxford University Press, Clarendon Press, 1969.

Finley, Moses I. "Crisis in the Classics." In *Crisis in the Humanities,* edited by J. H. Plumb. Baltimore: 1964.

Fisher, S. S., E. L. Gaden, O. A. Gianniny, Jr., L. A. Hoel. *Future Alternatives with Respect to the Division of Humanities in the School of Engineering and Applied Science.* Charlottesville, Va.: April 1984.

Flora, Peter, Arnold J. Heidenheimer, eds. *The Development of Welfare States in Europe and America*. New Brunswick: Transaction Books, 1981.

Florman, Samuel C. *The Civilized Engineer*. New York: St. Martin's Press, 1987.

———. *The Existential Pleasures of Engineering*. New York: St. Martin's Press, 1976.

Fuller, Timothy, ed. *The Voice of Liberal Learning: Michael Oakeshott on Education*. New Haven, Conn.: Yale University Press, 1989.

Gellner, Ernest. *Nations & Nationalism*. Ithaca, N.Y.: Cornell University Press, 1983.

Giovannelli, Leland. "Teaching Students How to Think for Themselves." In *American Society for Engineering Education, Proceedings* 1991, 2008–14.

Goethe, Johann Wolfgang von. *Faust*. Translated by C. F. MacIntyre. In *A Treasury of the Theatre*, edited by John Gassner. 3d ed. New York: Simon & Schuster, 1951.

Grafton, Anthony, Lisa Jardine. *From Humanism to the Humanities*. Cambridge, Mass.: 1986.

Hadas, Moses. *Old Wine, New Bottles: A Humanist Teacher at Work*. New York: Simon & Schuster, 1962.

Hamilton, Alexander, James Madison, John Jay. *The Federalist,* edited by Benjamin Fletcher Wright. Cambridge: Harvard University Press, Belknap Press, 1986.

Hammond, H. P. "Engineering Education After the War." *Toward an Engineering Education* 24, no. 9 (May 1944): 589–613.

Havel, Václav. *Disturbing the Peace*. New York: Knopf, 1990, 14.

Hirsch, Eric Donald, Jr. *Cultural Literacy: What Every American Needs to Know*. Boston: Houghton Mifflin, 1987.

Hirschman, Albert O. *The Passions and the Interests: Political Arguments for Capitalism Before Its Triumph*. Princeton: Princeton University Press, 1977.

Hochschild, Jennifer L. *What's Fair? American Beliefs About Distributive Justice*. Cambridge, Mass.: Harvard University Press, 1981.

Holstein, Edwin J., Earl D. McGrath. *Liberal Education and Engineering*. New York: Teachers' College, Columbia University, 1960.

Homer, *Iliad*. Edited by D. B. Munro and T. W. Allen. 3d ed. Oxford: Oxford University Press, 1920.

———. *Odyssey*. Edited by T. W. Allen. 2d ed. Oxford: Oxford University Press, 1917/19.

Horowitz, Donald L. *A Democratic South Africa? Constitutional Engi-*

neering in a Divided Society. Berkeley: University of California Press, 1991.

Hutchins, Robert Maynard. *The Great Conversation: The Substance of a Liberal Education.* Chicago: Encyclopedia Brittanica, 1952.

John-Paul II, Pope. *Laborem Exercens.* Vatican City: 1981.

Johnston, Joseph S., Jr., et al. *Unfinished Design: The Humanities and Social Sciences in Undergraduate Engineering Education.* Washington, D.C.: Association of American Colleges, 1988.

Kennan, George. "The Future of Professional Diplomacy." *Foreign Affairs* 33 (1954–1955): 566–67.

Kingsley, C. D., ed. *Cardinal Principles of Secondary Education: A Report of the Commission on the Reorganization of Secondary Education.* Appointed by the National Education Association. Bulletin, 1918, Washington, D.C.

Lakoff, Sanford A. "Schools and Democratic Values." *American Educator* (Summer 1981):15–19.

———. "The Third Culture." In *Knowledge and Power.* New York: Grove Press, 1966.

Laswell, Harold Dwight. *Who Gets What, When, How.* New York: McGraw Hill, 1936.

Leavis, F. R. *Two Cultures? The Significance of C. P. Snow.* London: Chatto & Windus, 1962.

Levine, George, Peter Brooks, et al. *Speaking for the Humanities.* American Council of Learned Societies, 1989. Occasional paper no. 7, New York: 1989.

The Liberties of the Massachusetts Collonie in New England, 1641.

Lijphart, Arend. *Democracies, Patterns of Majoritarian and Consensus Government in Twenty-One Countries.* New Haven, Conn.: Yale University Press, 1984.

———. *Democracy in Plural Societies.* New Haven, Conn.: Yale University Press, 1977.

Machiavelli, Niccolo. *The Prince.* Translated by Harvey C. Mansfield, Jr. Chicago: University of Chicago Press, 1985.

Mansfield, Harvey C., Jr. *America's Constitutional Soul.* Baltimore: Johns Hopkins Press, 1991.

Marx, Karl, Friedrich Engels. *The Communist Manifesto.* New York: International Publishers, 1948.

———. *On The Jewish Question.* In *Early Writings,* edited by T. B. Bottomore. London: Watts, 1963, 3–40.

Mill, John Stuart. *On Liberty.* In J. S. Mill, *Utilitarianism, Liberty and*

Representative Government, edited by E. Rhys. London: Everyman's Library, J. M. Dent & Sons, 1910.

Miller, Merle. *Plain Speaking: An Oral Biography of Harry S. Truman.* New York: Berkley Publishing Company, 1973.

Milton, John. *Tractate on Education.* Facsimile Ed. 1673, Oscar Browning, ed., Cambridge: 1895.

Montaigne, Michel de. *The Complete Essays of Montaigne.* Translated by D. Frame. Stanford: Stanford University Press, 1957.

Morison, Samuel Eliot. *Admiral of the Ocean Sea: A Life of Christopher Columbus.* 2 vols. Boston: Little Brown, 1942.

Mosteller, Frederick, Daniel Patrick Moynihan, eds. *On Equality of Educational Opportunity.* Papers deriving from the Harvard University Faculty Seminar on the Coleman Report. New York: Random House, 1972.

Moulakis, A. "The Value of Work." In *Sophia and Praxis: The Boundaries of Politics,* edited by Jene Porter. Chatham, N.J.: Chatham House, 1986.

Moynihan, Daniel Patrick. "Educational Goals and Political Plans." *Public Interest* (Winter 1991):32–48.

Naumann, Michael. *Der Abbau einer Verkeherten Welt.* Munich: List, 1969.

New York Times Magazine. October 20, 1991.

Oakeshott, Michael. "The Study of 'Politics' in a University." In *Rationalism in Politics.* Foreword by Timothy Fuller. New York: Methuen, 1981, 184–218.

Olmstead, Sterling P., et al. *Liberal Learning for the Engineer.* Washington, D.C.: American Society for Engineering Education, 1968.

Orwell, George. *1984.* New York: Dutton, 1949.

———. "Politics and the English Language." In *In Front of Your Nose, 1945–1950,* edited by Sonia Orwell and Ian Angus. Vol. 4 of *The Collected Essays, Journalism and Letters of George Orwell.* New York: Penguin, 1968, no. 38, 127–40.

Panel on Undergraduate Engineering Education (E. T. Cranch, Chairman), Committee on Education and Utilization of the Engineer. *Engineering Undergraduate Education.* Washington, D.C.: 1986.

Parsons, Talcott. "Change of Ethnicity." In *Ethnicity,* edited by Nathan Glazer and Daniel Patrick Moynihan. Cambridge, Mass.: Harvard University Press, 1975.

Pauling, Linus. "Scientists in Politics." In *The Place of Values in a World of Facts.* Proceedings of the Fourteenth Nobel Symposium, September 15–20, 1969. Edited by A. Tiselins, S. Nilsson. Stockholm: 1970, 197–205, 201.

Peters, Richard Starky. "Must an Education Have an Aim?" In *Concepts of Teaching: Philosophical Essays,* edited by C. J. B. Macmillan and Thomas W. Nelson. Chicago: Rand McNally, 1968, 89–98.

Plato. *Opera.* Edited by John Burnet. Oxford: Clarendon Press, 1905.

Professional Preparation Project of the Center for the Study of Higher and Postsecondary Education of the University of Michigan. *Professional/Liberal Undergraduate Self-Study PLUSS.* Ann Arbor: University of Michigan, 1990.

Richey, Russel E., Donald G. Jones, eds. *American Civil Religion.* New York: Harper & Row, 1974.

Robinson, Lou. "Disdain False Democracy." Review of Ellen Friedman and Miriam Fuchs, *Breaking the Sequence: Women's Experimental Fiction. American Book Review* (October–November 1991).

Rousseau, Jean-Jacques. *The Social Contract.* Translated by Maurice Cranston. London: Penguin, 1968.

Sale, Kirkpatrick. *The Conquest of Paradise.* New York: Knopf, 1990.

Samuel Neaman Institute of the Technion in Haifa. "Engineering Education 2001." *Engineering Education* (November 1987): 106–24.

Sartre, Jean-Paul. *Reflexions Sur la Question Juive.* Paris: Gallimard, 1954.

Schachterle, Lance. "WPI in the World: The WPI Global Project Program," *Interactions,* 10, Worcester, Mass.: 1989.

Schneider, David M. *American Kinship.* 2d ed. Chicago: University of Chicago Press, 1980.

Snow, C. P. *The Two Cultures; and a Second Look, an expanded version.* London: Cambridge University Press, 1969.

Sophocles. *Antigone,* edited with commentary by Richard C. Jebb. Cambridge: Cambridge University Press, 1902.

Sorenson, Theodore C. "America's First Post–Cold War President," *Foreign Affairs* (Fall 1992):13–30.

Stark, Joan S., Malcolm A. Lowther. *Strengthening the Ties That Bind: Integrating Undergraduate Liberal and Professional Study, Report of the Professional Preparation Network.* Ann Arbor: University of Michigan, 1988.

Steiner, George. *Language and Silence.* New York: Atheneum, 1967.

Taylor, Charles. *Sources of the Self.* Cambridge, Mass.: Harvard University Press, 1989.

Trow, Martin. "Problems in the Transition from Elite to Mass Higher Education." In *Policies for Higher Education.* Paris: UECD, 1974, 55–101. Reprint. Berkeley: Graduate School of Public Policy, University of California, 1975.

Van Doren, Mark. *Liberal Education.* Boston: Beacon Press, 1959.

Vico, Giambattista. *On the Study Method of Our Time.* Translated by Elio Gianturco. Indianapolis: Bobbs-Merrill, 1965.

Voegelin, Eric. *The New Science of Politics.* Chicago: University of Chicago Press, 1952.

Walker, E. A., J. M. Pettit, G. A. Hawkins. *Goals of Engineering Education, Final Report, the Goals Committee.* Washington, D.C.: American Society for Engineering Education, 1968.

Wall Street Journal (January 6, 1989).

Warren, Robert Penn. *Who Speaks for the Negro?* New York: Random House, 1965.

Weber, Max. *The Protestant Ethic and the Spirit of Capitalism.* Translated by Talcott Parsons. New York: Scribner, 1958.

Welch, John F., Jr., "Engineering and the Discipline of the Marketplace." *The Bridge* 18, no. 4 (Winter 1988): 2.

White, Robert M. "Of Walls and Bridges." *The Bridge* 19, no. 4 (Winter 1989–Spring 1990): 2–3.

Whitehead, Alfred North. *The Aims of Education and Other Essays.* New York: New American Library, 1959.

Wickenden, William Elgin. *Report of the Investigation of Engineering Education, 1923–1929.* Pittsburgh: Society of the Promotion of Engineering Education, vol. 1, 1930, vol. 2, 1934.

Wriston, Henry M. "Young Men in the Foreign Service." *Foreign Affairs* 33 (1954–1955): 28–42.

Zinn, Howard. *The People's History of the United States.* New York: Harper & Row, 1980.

Index

Abyssinia: 27
Academic disciplines: 117
Accreditation Board for Engineering and Technology (ABET): 127
Adler, Mortimer: ix
Aeneas: 84
Aeschylus: 56, 69
Aesthetics: 111
African art: 136
Alamo: 84
Albania: 27
Aleuts: 135
Alexandria: 85
Alfred P. Sloan School of Management: 20, 93
Alienation: 71, 74
Amateurs: 87
American Association for the Advancement of Science: 96, 105
American dream: 65
Amish: 49
Andrew Mellon Foundation: 23
Andromache: 141
Animal rights: 94
Antigone: 143
Anti-Semitism: 76
Apartheid: 52
Apollo: 55
Arendt, Hannah: 158
Aristotle: 45, 111, 112, 120, 142
Arnold, Matthew: 16
Art: 102, 111, 136, 137
Ascriptive bonds: 48, 73, 142
Assimilation: 74, 78, 135
AT&T: 12
Athens: 143
Atom bomb: 28, 62
Avant-garde: 77, 86
Aztecs: 67

Babel, Tower of: 41, 92, 105
Bacon, Francis: 19
Balkanization: 79

Barber, Benjamin: 54, 122
Barzun, Jacques: 153
Bell, Daniel: 146
Bellah, Robert: 149
Bellamy, Edward: 15
Bentham, Jeremy: 94
Bestor, Arthur: 149
Bible: 43, 56, 108
Black Power: 74
Blacks: 73
Blasphemers: 50
Bogner, Cindy: ix
Boniface VIII: 154
Boston: 74
Bourdieu, Pierre: 148
Boyer, Ernest: 145
Breughel, Pieter: 92
Brooklyn Bridge: 141
Burdell, Edwin S.: 156, 157
Burma: 27

California: 70, 80
Callicles: 118
Cannibals: 69
Capitalism: 66, 68, 72
Caribs: 67
Carmichael, Stokely (Kwame Ture): 75, 77, 86
Carter, Jimmy: 145
Ceausescu, Nicolae: 83
Celestine V: 154
Change: 22
Charlemagne: 82, 83
Cheit, Earl F.: 20, 146, 147
China: 52, 158
Chinese-Americans: 58
Cicero, M. Tullius: 56, 84
Cinco de Mayo: 48
Cipolla, Carlo M.: 151
Cities: 73
Citizenship: 23, 26, 142
Civil Rights: 74, 77
Civil Service: 120, 153, 154

Civil theology: American 42
Civilization: 42; Chinese, 58; familiarity with foreign, 64
Class: 15, 22, 34, 47, 58, 70, 74
Classics: 133; of science, 138
Cleaver, Eldridge: 77
Cleopatra: 84
Clough, David: ix
Colonial rule: 74
Columbia University: 121
Columbus, Christopher: 66
Columbus Day: 48
Communism: 27, 91
Community of learning: 122, 132
Comparative method: 69
Competitiveness: 30
Conformism: 85
Congress: 96
Consciousness-raising: 57, 71
Consensus juris: 50
Constitution: 43, 45
Conversation: 37, 56, 102, 131
Corruption: 96
Cortez, Hernan: 67
Counter-entropic groups: 78
Covenant: 43
Cranston, Maurice: ix
Culture: 32, 41, 46, 53, 70, 74, 78, 102
Cultures: 41, 42, 53, 57, 78, 100
Current events: 134
Curriculum: 5, 6, 105, 117, 126
Custom: 52, 73, 85
Czechoslovakia: 91
Czechs: 29

Dahrendorf, Ralf: 123–24
Danegeld: 147
Dante: 2, 154
Dartmouth College: 146
Deconstruction: 79
Defense: 60
Democracy: 23, 26, 32, 37, 122
Descartes, Rene: 66, 104
Determinism: 70, 75, 80, 86
Developing countries : 100
Dewey, John: 36
Dialectics: 71
Dionysius Areopagita: 56
Dionysus: 55
Discussion classes: 37, 122, 131
Diversity: 49, 85
Douglass, Frederick: 142

Durkheim, Emile: 43
Durrell, Lawrence: 85

École Polytechnique: 13
Eden: 66
Egypt: 85
Electoral campaigns: 108
Eliot, T. S.: 34, 155
Elizabeth II: 155
Engineering: and warfare, 13; preparation for useful occupations, 13; "self-justifying," 13; its logic, 47; pleasures of, 142
Engineering News and Railroad Journal: 13
English: 63, 108, 113
Equality: 23, 44, 86
Erasmus: 120
Ethics: 92, 110; "scientific," 94
Ethos: 43, 74
Euclid: 104
Europe: 63, 65, 78, 82, 135
European University Institute: 150
Europeans: 66, 76
Evans-Pritchard, E. E.: 152
Events of 1989: 27, 29
Everest: 101, 110
Experience: 87, 117, 139
Expertise: 1, 98, 102

Fajita-pita: 49
Family: 32
Fanon, Frantz: 73
Far East: 80; painting, 136
Faust: 144
Fetishism: 111
Fielding, Henry: 56
Finley, Moses I.: 56–57
Flora, Peter: 147
Florence: 16
Florman, Samuel: 110, 141
Foreign affairs: 60
Foreign study: 63
France: 42, 154
Freedom: 29, 65, 70, 91, 124, 142
Furs: 81

García Marquez, Federico: 54
Gellner, Ernest: 24, 43
Gender: 74, 80
Gentleman's C: 22
Germany: 42, 91
Giovannelli, Leland: ix, 157

God: 50, 143, 144
Gramsci, Antonio: 74
"Great Books": 56, 121
Greece, Ancient: 158; technology, 143
Greek-Americans: 46
Greek and Roman antiquity: 121
Greens: 96
Greenwich: 80

Hadas, Moses: 121
Harding, Warren: 62
Harvard University: 18; core curriculum, 119
Harvey Mudd College: 146
Havel, Vaclav: 91
Heidegger, Martin: 153
Heidenheimer, Arnold J.: 147
Herbst, Clarence: ix
Herbst Program of Humanities: ix, 5, 157
Heresy: 50
Herodotus: 69
Herzl, Theodor: 146
Hiroshima: 28
Hirsch, E. D.: 34, 41
Hirschman, Albert O.: 148
Hispanidad: 136
History: 27, 66, 82
Hitler, Adolf: 27, 80
Homer: 121
Hoover, Herbert: 145, 154
Horace: 121
Horton, Willie: 109
Humanism: 120
Hume, David: 55
Humpty Dumpty: 79, 80
Hungarian communities: 83
Hutchins, Robert M.: 32, 56, 122

IBM: 91
Ideas: 132
Identity: 57–58, 83, 117
Ideology: 68, 83
Immigrants: 33, 37, 46, 52, 69,
Incas: 67
Industrial society: 20, 26, 73
Ingenuity: 143
Irish: 46
Iron Curtain: 26
Isaiah: 72
Islamic Fundamentalism: 50
Isolationism: 60
Italians: 46

Ivory tower: 19

Jackson, Jesse: 77
Japan: 20, 33, 42, 49, 63
Jefferson, Thomas: 65, 123
Jews: 76, 152
Job: 136
John-Paul II: 158
Judgment: 106, 120, 127
Junkerman, Charles: 118, 151
Justice and utility: 4

Kant, Immanuel: 55
Kennan, George: 61
King, Martin Luther, Jr.: 74, 108
Kingsley, C. D. : 149
Kraus, Karl: 80
Kremlin: 26
Kuwait: 52

Labor: dignity of, 141
Lakoff, Sanford A.: ix, 149, 154
Land grant colleges: 15, 54
Language: 3, 12, 22, 31, 43, 50, 51,
    55, 63, 70, 79, 104, 108, 109, 123
Last move: fallacy of, 28
Latin: 154
Lawrence, D. H.: 44
Law: 41, 45, 51, 53
Lawyers: 98
Learning: 34, 37, 133
Leavis, F. R.: 154
Lebanon: 78
Leibnitz, G. F. von: 104
Leisure: 142
Lenin, V. I.: 86
Lesseps, Ferdinand de: 47
Leviticus: 150
Liberation: 89, 97, 98
Liberties of Massachussetts: 50
Liberty: 29, 91
Life-styles: 51, 85
Literacy: 23; cultural, 32; scientific
    and technical, 97
Literature: 101, 133
Locke, John: 118
Los Angeles: 76
Louvre: 58

Machiavelli, Nicolo: 80
Managerialism: 99
Mansfield, Harvey C., Jr.: ix, 150
Maori: 135

Marcuse, Herbert: 91
Marx, Karl: 69
Marxism: 27, 70, 80
Mathemetics: 105
Mayas: 67
Mayflower: 84
McMuffin: 26
Mephistopheles: 144
Mexico: 66
Military academies: 13
Mill, John Stuart: 85, 87
Milton, John: 112
Missionaries: 100
MIT: 18, 20, 23, 93
Mondale, Walter: 109
Montaigne, Michel de: 69
Morrill Act: 15
Morris, William: 13
Moynihan, Daniel P.: 33
Multinational corporations: 91

Naples: 93
National Academy of Engineering:
    26, 30
National communities: 42
National personality: attachment to,
    30, 42, 82
Nationalism: 82
Nativism: 46
Natural Science: 121
Naumann, Michael: 152
Netherlands: 78
New Left: 73
Newman, Cardinal John: 17, 18
Nimrod: 41
Noah's Ark: 84
Nobel, Alfred: 146

Oakeshott, Michael: 155
Oedipus complex: 76
Office of Technology Assessment: 96
Olmstead, Sterling P.: 128
Oppenheimer, J. Robert: 104, 118
Ordinary life: affirmation of, 141.
Orwell, George: 80
Otherness: 50, 52

Pacific Rim: 80, 135
Panama: 52
Paris: 80
Parochialism: 60, 136
Parthenon: 143
Pauling, Linus: 94

Peace: 26
Peace Corps: 63
Pearl Harbor: 60
Pei, I. M.: 58
Penelope: 141
Persians: 69
Personality: 31
Peru: 149
Philistinism: 19, 118, 129
Philosophy: 102, 118; and technology,
    141
Plato: 54, 118, 141, 143
Pliny: 121
Politics: 97, 111
Poor Richard's Almanack: 16
Popularizing: 118
Pre-Columbian America: 67
Productivity: 19
Property: 51, 70
Psychoanalytic theories: 74
"Publius": 78
Puritan work ethic: 92
Pursuit of happiness: 85, 142
Pushkin, Alexander: 56

Quebecois: 78

Race: 93
Racism: 54, 86
Recognition: 70, 85
Relativism: 51
Relevance: 17, 135
Renaissance: 120
Revolution: 71
Rights: 45, 51, 51, 91
Rimini, Francesca da: 2
Riots: 76
Roebling, J. A. and W. A.: 141
Rogers, Barton: 18
Romania: 83
Romans: 84
Romulus: 84
ROTC: 17, 118
Rousseau, Jean-Jacques: 4
Rust Belt: 22
Rutherford, E.: 101

Sade, D. A. F. de: 55
Saint John's College: ix, 121
Saint John's Gospel: 144
Saint-Simon, Henri de: 146
Salamis: 69
Sartre, Jean-Paul: 76

SAT scores: 128
Sawyer, Diane: 58
Schachterle, Lance: 151
Schools: 32, 93, 108, 126
Science: 3, 93, 100, 105, 125
Scientists: 94
Scipio Africanus: 84
Scoda: 91
SDI: 28, 60
Seebass, Richard: ix
Sexism: 80
Shakespeare: 101
Shelley, Percy Bysshe: 56
Slavery: 142
Snobbery: 86, 142
Snow, C. P.: 93, 100
Social cohesion: 4, 42, 79
Socialization: 48
Sophocles: 141
South Africa: 52, 78
Soviet Empire: 29
Soviet Latvia: 52
Spellcheckers: 107
Sputnik: 5
Stanford, Leland: 15, 20
Stanford, Leland, Jr.: 16
Stanford University: 75, 118, 150, 151
State Department: 61
Steiner, George: 108
Sterne, Lawrence: 56
Stevens, Wallace: 124
Strauss, Leo: 153
Suez Canal: 47
Sununu, John: 145
Supreme Court: 45
Suttner, Bertha von: 146
Switzerland: 49, 78
Syncretism: 49

Tarantella: 48
Tarquin: 84
Taste: 120
Taylor, Charles: 158
Teachers: 2, 36, 129–30, 132
Teaching: 32, 36; and research 128, 132
Technology: 1, 26, 60, 91
Television: 108
Tennyson, Alfred Lord: 28; *Mechanophilus,* 17, 146; *Locksley Hall,* 28
Textbooks: 106, 120, 133
Texts: 54, 133; narrative, 136; dramatic, 137; analytic, 138; introspective, 138
Thatcher, Margaret: 154
Thayer School: 146
Thermodynamics: Second Law of, 100, 140
Thomas Aquinas, Saint: 144
Thucydides: 121
Tibet: 27
Tienanmen Square: 27, 52
Time: 84
Tocqueville, Alexis de: 44, 79
Tokenism: 58
Toleration: 49, 85
Touchstone Project, CZM: 158
Tradition: 54; Western, 135
Trow, Martin: 147
Troy: 141
Truman, Harry: 28

Ulysses: 144
United Nations: 28
United States: myths, 65
University: 17, 57, 59, 121, 122, 125, 140
University of Colorado: ix, 5, 149, 156, 157
University of Virginia: 157

Values: 5, 16, 30, 52, 110
Van Doren, Mark: 112
Vargas-Llosa, Mario: 149
Vico, Giambattista: 92, 104
Violence: 71, 77, 99
Voegelin, Eric: 149
Voltaire, F. M. A. de: 56

Washington, George: 62, 65, 84
Watts: 74
Weber, Max: 50, 92
Welch, John F., Jr.: 30
West Point: 13
White, Robert M.: 26
Whitehead, Alfred North: 19
Worcester Polytechnic Institute: 151
Word: 104; and Deed 141
World economy: 60
Wriston, Henry M.: 151
Writing: 139

Xenophobia: 61
Xenophon: 56